DAVID P. MCINTYRE
BECAUSE THEY SAID SO ISN'T GOOD ENOUGH

WorkBook PRESS

Copyright @2020 by David P. McIntyre

All rights reserved. No part of this book may be reproduced in any form or by any electronic or mechanical means, including information storage and retrieval systems, without permission in writing from the publisher, except by reviewers, who may quote brief passages in a review.

This publication contains the opinions and ideas of its author. It is intended to provide helpful and informative material on the subjects addressed in the publication. The author and publisher specifically disclaim all responsibility for any liability, loss or risk, personal or otherwise, which is incurred as a consequence, directly or indirectly, of the use and application of any of the contents of this book.

WORKBOOK PRESS LLC
187 E Warm Springs Rd,
Suite B285, Las Vegas, NV 89119, USA

Website:	https://workbookpress.com/
Hotline:	1-888-818-4856
Email:	admin@workbookpress.com

Ordering Information:
Quantity sales. Special discounts are available on quantity purchases by corporations, associations, and others.
For details, contact the publisher at the address above.

Library of Congress Control Number:
ISBN-13:   978-1-952754-91-3 (Paperback Version)
            978-1-952754-92-0 (Digital Version)

REV. DATE: 10/09/2020

For details , contact the author at the address below.
dpmcintyre1@outlook.com

All Biblical references are based on the New King James Version.

PROLOGUE

"Because They Said So Isn't Good Enough"

Remember when your children were young? We could not wait until the kids could talk. We tried to get them to say certain words and make sentences. We asked them questions and wondered at their responses. Then they got older. First, we heard the word, "No", then we began hearing a different word, "Why". Asking why is not wrong; in fact, it is part of growing up and how they gather information. After a while though, we simply get tired of the why's and we try to stop further questions by pulling out the old-worn phrase "Because I said so, that's why".

Sometimes, "Because I said so" responses work if we have authority over the child and the child respects and trusts the one saying it. It rarely satisfies, however. We may go a long time before the "Because I said so" phrase is challenged, even well into adulthood. At some point, if we are to believe something is true, the question "Why?" must be answered. We may tell our children, for example, to believe in Santa Claus. They may accept Santa as real for a time, but unless we can prove him to be real, eventually they will know he is just a nice tradition.

I was the same way when it came to science. I accepted whatever was said in the textbooks without question. As I grew older, I wanted to know how things worked. I began to read textbooks on my own to discover more facts about my world. In learning new things, I developed a kind of awe for the scientists that figured out how all the world worked. It was only natural that I took all the science and math classes I could in high school and college. In math classes, I demanded that things be proven before I would accept them and the same was true in physics and chemistry. Curiously though, I accepted whatever was in the biology textbooks as absolute fact. This included the theory of evolution and I did not doubt what I was taught. They said it was so, so it had to be so. I was more interested in physics and math than biology anyway.

After college graduation, I became a teacher. One summer while teaching several science subjects, including biology, a student challenged me asking, "Why do I have to learn about evolution when I don't believe in it?". I was incredulous! In fact, I was angry that this uneducated young man would dare to challenge the prevailing scientific theory and me personally as his teacher. I was so angry, in fact, another teacher had to step in and talk to us both so we could get the class back on track.

After that incident, I was determined to study all the evidence that proved evolution to be true. If I was ever confronted again, I planned to blow away their obvious ignorance with a rapid-fire barrage of solid evidence absolutely proving evolution true. As I searched the evidence, I could not find the proof I sought and was dumbfounded! In my search I found many people saying evolution was true and who seemed to delight in ridiculing anyone who questioned the theory. In fact, there seemed to be, and still is, an unwillingness to allow open debate so that people can make up their own minds after hearing all the evidence. That attitude really disturbed me. Even when I found "so-called" proof I was disappointed because:

- Not all the evidence was presented, and the complete evidence was often better explained in terms of intelligent design rather than random changes.

- It was impossible for natural processes to produce the change and yet a supernatural cause was ignored.

- Evidence was falsified or twisted to make it appear as if the theory of evolution was true.

I searched for about a year and could not find one form of proof that I could state absolutely proved evolution to be true. I was shocked! Even worse (or better depending on how you view it) I found the explanations based on creative design by an all-powerful God more satisfying and (dare I say it) more scientific! Therefore, by an "evolutionary" process I became a creationist.

That was over 40 years ago. Though retired now, I was an instructor for laser-based medical instruments used in cancer, AIDS and other forms of research. Most of my students were MD's and PhD's and many of them also expressed a disbelief in evolution. In all those years, I have not found any new arguments or evidence that would change my mind back to believing in evolution. In fact, I have found a lot more evidence pointing toward a creator God! I came to realize that the only reason that I believed in the theory of evolution was because the textbooks said so. That reason is not good enough anymore. I hope it isn't good enough for you either. I hope you will take the time to read on and let me show you what I learned.

Table of Contents

Chapter 1 – *Evolution: Fact or Faith*..9

Chapter 2 – *Life: How Complex is the Problem?*..............................27

Chapter 3 – *Overcoming the Odds:*
               Does Nature Really have the Tools?......................39

Chapter 4 – *Aren't There Proofs That Evolution is True?*.................51

Chapter 5 – *I Heard They Created Life in The Laboratory*...............69

Chapter 6 – *All Those Fossils Prove*
               Evolution is True, Don't They?..............................79

Chapter 7 – *Dating and Time*...105

Chapter 8 – *Living Challenges*...127

Chapter 9 – *Put It All Together*..137

Epilogue – *A Different Perspective from Genesis 1*.......................139

David P. Mcintyre

CHAPTER 1 – Evolution: Fact or Faith

First Some Ground Rules...

I remember years back having a very heated discussion with a fellow worker in the office about how one of our instruments operated. At the time we were both instructors for a medical instrument company that produced cellular analysis instruments used in hospital and research labs. Our decibel levels got louder and louder and some of the office workers were sure we were going to come to blows over our disagreement. After a time, we each listened a bit more closely to what the other person was saying. We discovered we really did not disagree after all yet simply had not defined the problem. When we did, we found we were both right. Under a certain set of circumstances, he was correct and under a different set of circumstances I was correct. We walked away friends, even joking about it, but that did not stop the talk around the office for a while. You see, we had failed to clearly define what we were talking about. Had we done so, we may have solved the disagreement much sooner and with far less concern from our fellow workers.

We need to do the same thing before we discuss evolution; first, clearly define what we mean by evolution. A clear definition gives us a starting point. The definition must also include within it a means to determine whether something fits it or not. If we defined a rock, for example, as any hard object, then a desk is a rock. A car is a rock. A book is a rock. A dog for that matter is a rock (try running into one!). You can see that the definition is too general.

Some, I believe, make the same mistake when defining evolution. They define the theory as simply "change". If a car gets into an accident and is now changed, does that mean the car has evolved? We grow older and our hair color turns gray. We have changed, but have we really evolved? Someone gets cancer. Someone dies. A building collapses. These are examples of change, but no one would point to any of these as evolution expressed in the biology textbooks. We need a better definition.

Webster's dictionary defines evolution as:

"The gradual process of development or change;"[1]

---
1 *Webster's Classic Reference Library* (Ashland, Ohio: Landoll, Inc., 1999).

Because They Said So Isn't Good Enough

This definition is still too broad because it does not give us a means to discern whether a change indicates something is evolving or devolving. How about the following:

"A process of continuous change from a lower, simpler or worse to a higher, more complex, or better state."

Now we test our observations against the definition. Cars getting into accidents, people getting cancer, or a building collapsing would not fit the definition of a change to a better state. On the other hand, a modern car as compared to the early Model T clearly exhibits evolution to a more complex or better state.

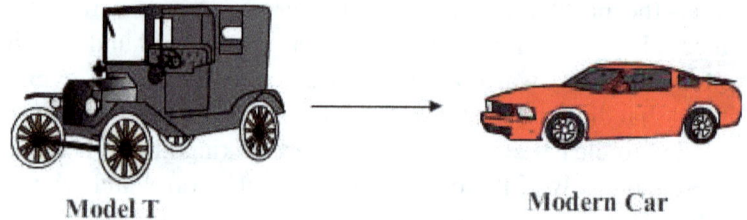

Model T   Modern Car

(Note: The only way cars evolved was as a result of highly intelligent scientists and engineers developing improvements to the basic car design)

The biology textbooks basically describe particles to man changes over time.

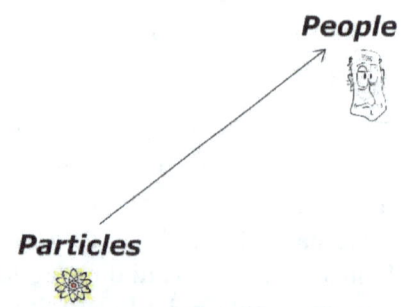

The key is understanding that the theory of evolution does not simply mean change. A change that does not exhibit upward movement to a higher more complex organism does not fit the definition. It cannot, therefore, be used as proof of evolution. We need to keep this definition in mind when we later look at the "so-called" evidence proving evolution true.

While we discuss definitions, let us also define what we mean by science since evolution is often considered a science.

Webster's dictionary defines science as:

"A possession of knowledge as distinguished from ignorance or misunderstanding, knowledge attained through study or practice"[2]

Did you get that? Knowledge is obtained by study, by observing the world around us. At the beginning of every science textbook is a discussion of "The Scientific Method". It describes the approach to gathering information that ultimately leads to scientific discoveries. The following diagram roughly illustrates that process:

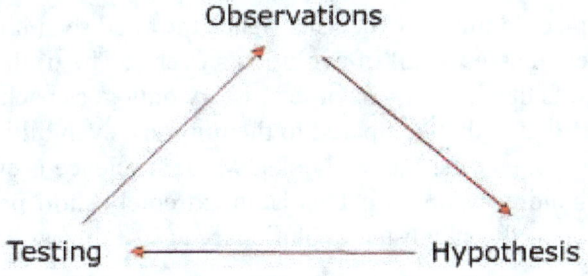

The idea is to make careful observations of our world that, in turn, should lead to a hypothesis explaining what we see. The hypothesis may be right or wrong, so a series of tests are devised. The tests generate new observations that either confirms the hypothesis, negates it or indicates it needs some work. We might, for example, observe leaves and branches falling to the ground. The branches seem to come crashing down when they fall while the leaves float gently to the ground. We hypothesize that a difference in weight makes the branch fall faster than the leaf. In trying to "prove" our hypothesis, we drop two stones, one about the weight of the leaf, and the other about the weight of our branch. If our hypothesis is correct, the heavier stone should clearly fall faster than the lighter one. When we drop the stones (reproducing Galileo's famous experiment), we find they hit the ground at the same time. Our hypothesis is wrong! There must be something else besides weight creating the falling speed difference. If we observe long enough, we will understand the effects of surface area and air resistance on the falling speed. This is how science is

---

2   Ibid.

supposed to work.

How About an Eyewitness...

Many scientists (although not all) are adamant that the world evolved, and that no Creator was involved at all. They feel the theory of evolution is a proven fact and all those who disagree must be ignorant fools.

> *"O Timothy! Guard what was committed to your trust, avoiding profane and idle babblings and contradictions of what is falsely called knowledge."* (1 Tim 6:20)

> *"The fool has said in his heart there is no God."* (Psalm 14:1)

You would think by their insistence they had seen it all and could speak as eyewitnesses of all of evolution's events. The truth, however, is that no one was there. Man's recorded history only goes back about 6,000 years or so. What is that compared to the millions, even billions, of years of evolution spoken of in the textbooks? Modern science is even younger, only a few hundred years old. This is an extremely short period of time in comparison to the suggested evolutionary age of the earth of about 4.5 billion years.

Just how short is the time?

If we imagine that one 24-hour period represents the supposed age of the earth, 4.5 billion, then recorded history would only be .12 seconds out of the entire day. That is less than one blink of an eye. Modern science would be less than a tenth of that time or less than .01 second! Dear reader, that is like trying to discern a full day's worth of activities in a fraction of the time it takes to blink and then concluding how the entire day has gone.

David P. Mcintyre

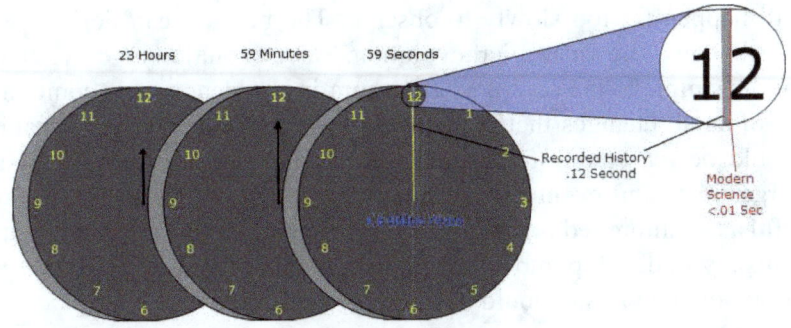

We have observed our world for an extremely short period of time. Is this enough time to be certain of any conclusions? Try this experiment for yourself: Flip open a magazine for just a fraction of a second. Now write on paper everything you saw on that page. Once you have done that, come up with a plausible way the magazine produced itself based on what you have observed.

Sound a bit farfetched? I agree but isn't that exactly what we have done with our evolution conclusions? We have essentially observed a relatively finished Earth and then made claims on how it produced itself. In the magazine analogy, we may come up with some interesting and very imaginative ways the paper might have produced itself and believe them to be true. All of which would be fantasy ignoring the creative process of another human being producing the page. Such conclusions require faith and an incredible amount at that! We cannot observe the evolutionary process directly even if true. The first step in the scientific method cannot be applied.

How About a Test...

A hypothesis is reasonable if there is corroborating evidence through testing. I cannot observe your brain directly, for example, but I can observe your behavior or talk with you and thus conclude that you must have a brain. What kind of corroborating tests can be made in support of a "faith" that evolution is true?

Have we ever really seen a large change, known as macroevolution? Has anyone ever seen a fish change to an amphibian, an amphibian to a mammal or a lizard into a bird? The answer is no. Not even in all the scientific experiments has anyone observed such a change. If it occurs, it will happen far too slowly to observe. The best we can do is observe small changes, known as microevolution. Since evolution involves change from the simple to the complex, corroborating evidence must come in the form of small changes that collectively appear to improve the organism. It would be reasonable to assume that small, good changes might lead to larger ones and eventually to a new organism. However, we must be careful as an improved organism can be just that. It does not mean that the organism will develop into a new more complex organism. Without direct observation, that again would be a leap of faith.

Evolutionists also assume that changes (microevolution) is exclusive to the evolutionary viewpoint. If God created the world, could He not also build into the creation the ability to change? Why wouldn't an all mighty God program His creation to adapt to changes that occur such as, changes in weather or climate. How about to adapt to changes in food supply? How about changes just to provide variety? The Bible speaks of changes in climate, changes in man's lifespan and changes in animal coloration, just to name a few. When you buy a car, you are given choices: color, engine size, upgrade options, etc. Could God do the same thing? The changes would be limited. There are only so many colors, so many engine sizes, so many options and there would only be so many changes allowed for a type of living thing.

The Bible indicates that there are separate kinds of living things and they cannot interbreed because they are separate kinds of flesh.

> *"All flesh is not the same flesh, but there is one kind of flesh of men, another flesh of animals, another of fish, and another of birds."* (1 Cor 15:39)

Now we have a way to prove evolution over creation! Just record a video of a fish becoming an amphibian, a reptile becoming a bird or how about a monkey turning into a man. Evolution says it can happen; the Bible indicates it cannot. The problem is that it has never been observed and without observation and rigorist testing evolution becomes just a hypothesis. A hypothesis without observation and testing is really an assumption; something you believe is true without proof. You may be able to reason with that assumption, but you cannot say that it is true or false. If you say something is true based only on an assumption, are you speaking from science or faith?

To be fair, creation is also a hypothesis. If in fact God did it, no one was there to observe it. He would have to tell us He did it and any details He cared to share as to how He did it. The Bible also indicates that He finished the creation (Genesis 1) so we cannot test it.

> *"In the beginning God created the heavens and the earth."* (Genesis 1:1)

> *"And on the seventh day God ended His work which He had done and rested on the seventh day from all His work which He had done."* (Genesis 2:2)

Fact or Faith?

The absence of direct proof means these two hypotheses are both beliefs. Whichever you choose to believe in is your choice whether it is evolution or creation or some combination of the two. None of these can be observed directly and therefore are beyond direct scientific proof. The only thing we can do is gather circumstantial evidence and see which model fits the evidence the best and then make our choice. We will look at some of the circumstantial evidences later in this book. Even then, our personal biases may influence our choice. Those rejecting that God exists, for example, will automatically reject any evidence pointing to creation. Others, who accept God, may misconstrue their own personal biases as absolute truth. Such attitudes are unfortunate and not in keeping with the spirit of true science. New evidence, even circumstantial, should cause us to reevaluate our original hypothesis.

I know for those of us that have a high regard for science (and I include myself in this group) the idea that science cannot prove our origin is tough. We would like to think that science can solve all problems and answer all the riddles of life, but some are beyond scientific investigation. Like it or not, the answers will require a step of faith.

The Laws of Science – Do They Point Us to Evolution?

In the absence of direct observable proof, the best we can do is observe the laws of science and see if they point us toward evolution. Some of these laws, the law of gravity or Newton's laws of motion, are neutral. They may suggest, for example, why bigger animals must have stronger legs (e.g. to overcome gravity) but they do not tell us how the animal got that way. Did the animal evolve or did a supreme intelligence create bigger legs knowing the need? The law of gravity cannot answer the question. The laws of thermodynamics, however, tell us something of the general rules under which our universe seems to operate. These rules give us a clue to whether our universe is evolving or not. There are two laws generally referred to in the textbooks.

> ***The first law*** basically states that in everything we observe the sum of matter and energy remains constant.

All Interactions

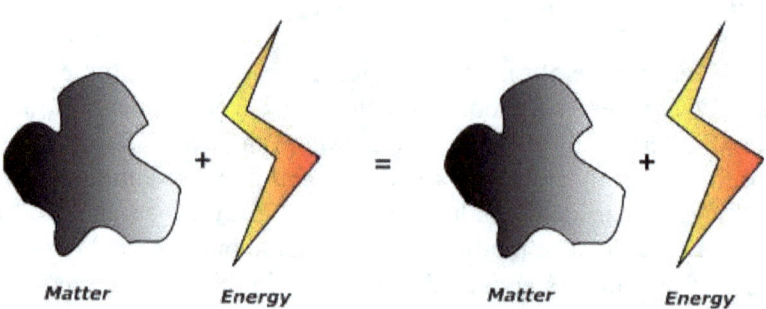

Matter Energy Matter Energy

So how do these laws relate to our discussion? In the first law we observe matter being converted into energy (the atomic bomb is an example) and vice versa. In every reaction, the total amount of matter and energy remains the same. We never observe matter being produced from nothing. We never observe energy coming from nothing. Then where did matter come from? The first law tells us that the universe could not have created itself. To do so means that something would have had to be produced from nothing. The conclusion, then, is that something outside of the universe created it or that the universe is eternal. God did it or it has always been there.

The atheist does not accept that God exists and will claim that the universe is eternal. He will claim:

1. I believe there is no God or,
2. There is no God

I would accept the first statement. It is an honest assessment of their world view. I do have a problem with the second statement. I believe it is unrealistic. Consider this, have you ever searched for someone from room to room while they are moving room to room as well? You might easily miss each other because while you are in one room, they are in another. You could only eliminate that they are not in the building if you could search all the rooms at the same time. For someone to say that there is no God, they would have to be able to go into every corner and dimension of the entire universe simultaneously and record that there is no God anywhere. That person would have to be omniscient, omnipotent, and omnipresent to do such a thing. They would have to be God to disprove the existence of God. The first statement is an honest expression of belief. The second statement does not recognize the limits of human ability. In either case, they are acting in and expressing faith.

> ***The second law*** states that in all observable reactions the tendency is toward a higher more disordered entropy state.

If you believe that matter is eternal, the second law is a problem. It says the tendency of the universe is toward disorder. If you buy a new car, does the car get better and better over time or does it begin to fail, fade, and rust? If you build a new house, does the house improve with age or does it require attention and maintenance? The observed tendency is downward not upward, worse not better over time. If the universe is eternal, then it should have worn itself out a long time ago. The car can only last so long and then it is useless. The best-built house will eventually crumble. Many scientists have pondered this dilemma and proposed that the universe should eventually suffer a "heat death", a point where there is no longer any useful energy left and no way to produce any.

Heat Death

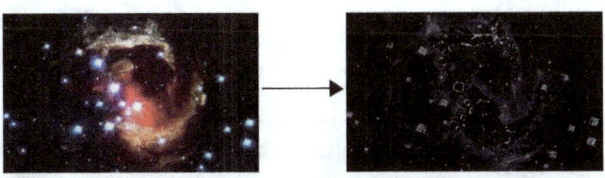

No useful energy

In everything we do, we use up useful energy. Matter stored with a lower entropy state must be sacrificed. Gasoline is burned. Wood is set ablaze and reduced to ash. Other things must be used up to produce electricity, which itself is used up. While the sum of the matter and energy of the universe remains constant (1st law) the usefulness of such conversions decreases over time (2nd law). If the universe is eternal, we should not even be having this discussion. The universe should have died a long time ago.

When Hubble studied the heavens through his telescope, he made a startling discovery.

There is a definite shift of light toward the red end of the spectrum coming from the distant stars. The shift is referred to as a doppler shift. The idea is like the sound change we hear as a train or vehicle approaches our position and then moves away.

Doppler Sound Shift

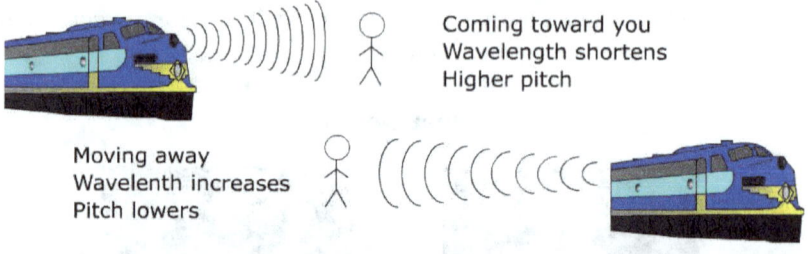

Coming toward you
Wavelength shortens
Higher pitch

Moving away
Wavelenth increases
Pitch lowers

The sound waves of an approaching train are bunched tighter together, and the pitch will be higher. As the train moves away, the sound waves are pulled farther apart and the pitch lowers. Light also appears to have wave-like characteristics. Light from distant stars moving away from us will have the light wavelengths stretched, shifting the color toward the red longer wavelengths.

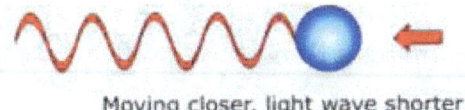

Moving closer, light wave shorter

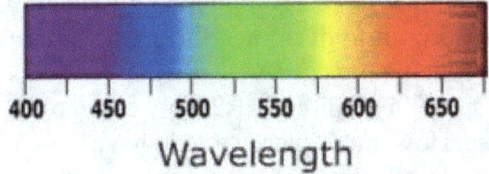

Moving away, light waves longer

Light Spectrum

400   450   500   550   600   650

Wavelength

The conclusion was that the universe appears to be expanding in all directions like an inflated balloon.

Expanding Universe

It also meant that if you go back in time, the universe had a beginning! This was a bombshell to the scientific community because the prevailing theory was that the universe had always existed and was in a steady state. In formulating his famous theory of relativity, Einstein came to the same conclusion. He, in fact, thought he was wrong and inserted a constant into his equation to counteract the "error". Later, he realized the theory was correct and removed the constant.[3]

---

3   Henry F. Schaefer, Science and Christianity: Conflict or Coherence? (Athens GA, University of Georgia Printing Department, 2016). P. 46.

Solve the Problem with a Bomb?

Many scientists recognizing the problem with the laws of thermodynamics have postulated that the universe began with a "big bang". The idea is that the universe is cyclic. Periodically, (billions of years in between), they believe that gravity pulls everything together into one huge mass in a small volume creating tremendous heat. The mass then explodes sending matter in all directions and the universe begins again. There are some scientists that suggest such action would be impossible because the outward exploding force, they calculate, is not enough to overcome the tremendous gravitational forces. A tremendous amount of energy must be expended for a spacecraft to overcome the earth's gravitational force and enter space. How much more energy would have to be used to explode the entire earth into space in all directions? Now extrapolate in your thinking the entire universe. How much energy would have to be used to blow apart the entire universe in all directions and overcome the gravitational force of that same universe? The calculations approach the infinite. Even if such an event could have happened, it still does not answer the question of the second law of thermodynamics. The general tendency of the universe is toward a more disordered state. This would mean that a "big bang" would not only have to blow everything apart but would also have to increase the order in the universe.

Let me insert an analogy here to make the point. Suppose you buy a piece of property, clear it, and then proceed to build a new house on the site. In the process of clearing the land, laying a foundation, building the walls, adding plumbing and electrical and finally finishing the house, you are transforming the site from a less ordered to a more ordered state. From then on, the house tends toward a more disordered state as it wears out and needs repair. It reaches an extreme state of disorder when it crumbles. Now, how many of you would expect to build the house by blowing up a piece of property piled up with rocks, wood, glass, and other materials? As for me, I do not have enough faith to believe that is possible because bombs do not build things. They destroy things. Would a "big bang" build order or disorder?

Many people over the years have speculated on how the explosion of the universe may have come together into galaxies, solar systems, planets, and moons to set the stage for the "evolution" of life. I believe they largely ignore the 2nd law of thermodynamics or relegate it to an insignificant influence on the process. Since the law appears to be so universal, I believe this is a mistake. We fail to recognize that this speculation is just that, speculation. It has not been observed. Even if it did occur, it would have happened long before man was even around. Are they then speaking from established scientific fact or from faith?

OK, Let's Compromise...

At first glance, a compromise between the two opposing viewpoints of evolution and pure creation might seem the best solution. Many certainly do express that belief. We must remember, though, this compromise is not a compromise of science and religion but of one belief with another belief producing a third belief. We cannot prove scientifically our origin hypotheses.

Such compromises usually do not satisfy everyone. To those who believe strongly that the Bible is God's Word, reject the idea of "worshipping and serving the creature more than the Creator". To the naturalist who wants to explain everything without God, he/she will have trouble putting God in the picture. What part did He do? What part just evolved?

For example, two of the most often repeated compromises are the "Day Age" theory and the "Gap" theory. In the first theory, the days of Genesis are interpreted to be long time periods representing the long ages required for an evolutionary process. This theory is based on 2 Peter 3:8 (NKJV):

> *"... that with the Lord one day is as a thousand years, and a thousand years as one day."*

Because They Said So Isn't Good Enough

The Gap theory stuffs the long time period required for evolution between Genesis 1:1 and Genesis 1:2. In this theory, evolution struggled for a while and then God stepped in and redid it all. Do these compromises really help? I do not think so. The Bible-believer continuously struggles with how to fit these ideas in with the Scripture passages. Those that could care less about the Bible, have no need to compromise with it. The atheist will not compromise because he does not believe in God. It should be said that the compromisers are often believers in God attempting to reach out to those that do not believe. The believer may believe in either creation or some form of evolution. The atheist must believe only in evolution; he cannot compromise. Which then of the two is trying to be more open minded?

There is a problem with fitting evolution into the wording of the Scriptures. Suppose you are the writer of a book. When you are finished, do you want people to understand your viewpoint or would you want someone to use your words to justify a viewpoint diametrically opposed to yours? I think the answer is obvious. You would want to choose your words so carefully as to not be misunderstood. If God is the writer of the Bible, and I believe He is, I think He would do the same. For example, if He wished to convey the idea, He created the world in six literal days, what words would he use?

I believe that the best Hebrew word to use to mean one day is the word "Yom". Dr. Henry Morris, a scientist and Bible scholar, had this to say about the Hebrew word "Yom" translated "day" in Genesis 1:

> *"There is no doubt that Yom can be used to express time in a general sense. In fact, it is translated as 'time' in the King James translation 65 times. On the other hand, it is translated as 'day' almost 1200 times. In addition, its plural form yamen is translated as 'days' approximately 700 times. It is obvious, therefore, that the normal meanings of Yom and yam in are 'day' and 'days,' respectively. If a parabolic or metaphorical meaning is intended, it is made obvious in the context. In approximately 95% of its occurrences, the literal meaning is intended."*[4]

Further on he states:

---

4   Henry M. Morris. *Scientific Creationism* (San Diego, CA: Creation-Life Publishers, 1974). p. 223.

> *"It might still be contended that, even though Yom never requires the meaning of a long age, it might possibly permit it. However, the writer of the first chapter of Genesis has very carefully guarded against such a notion, both by modifying the noun by a numerical adjective ('first day,' 'second day,' etc.), and also by indicating the boundaries of the time period in each case as "evening and morning."*[5]

Language certainly is not as exact as pure math, but I believe if you choose a word most often meaning a literal day, define a day as the "evening and the morning" six times and number the days (Genesis 1:5, 8, 13, 19, 23 and 31), the meaning is a literal day. Now we may attempt to allegorize Genesis or reject it but let us at least realize the simplest, clearest interpretation is that of a literal day! In 2 Peter 3:8, the passage makes no sense unless a day means a day:

> *"... that with the Lord one day is as a thousand years, and a thousand years as one day."*

Or,

> *"...that with the LORD a long age is as a thousand years, and a thousand years as a long age."*

There are some that claim that Genesis cannot mean a literal day because it takes much longer than a day for plants to grow and mature and meet the requirement that they be fruitful and can multiply. I disagree. I believe that in the beginning God created fully formed, mature plants and animals within the specified days. He did so with Adam and Eve. I believe that God is not limited by time as He created it. I do not agree that Genesis teaches that we are still in the 7th day. It says that God rested on the 7th day because He had finished all His work of creation (Genesis 2:2). The 6-day work week followed by a day of rest became the pattern for us to follow.

> *"Six days you shall do your work, and on the seventh day you shall rest, that your ox and your donkey may rest, and the son of your female servant and the stranger may be refreshed."* (Exodus 23:12)

I sincerely doubt that later references to working 6 days followed by a day of rest (such as the one just quoted) means that we only work 6 days and then rest indefinitely. It just means we should take a day (one 24-hour period) of rest before starting another work week.

---

5   Ibid.

There are spiritual problems with the compromise positions. How would you like to be punished before doing anything wrong? You see spiritually God did not curse the ground, bringing death into the world, until Adam and Eve sinned (Genesis 3:17). With the "Day Age" and the "Gap" theory death is present long before man sinned. Living things would have struggled and died in the evolution process leading up to fallen man. If evolution existed before man fell, why then would God say the earth was now going to groan and travail after man sinned? The earth had already groaned and travailed! Either God is very cruel, or He meant what He said. He created the earth "very good" in the beginning and only after man's fall did punishment come. He punished after sin not before.

The creation order is different in the evolution model as compared to the Genesis account. Observe the chart below:

<u>Creation</u>	<u>Evolution</u>
1. Heavens, earth, light, darkness	1. Sun, moon, stars
2. Air, water, canopy	2. Land, water
3. Dry land, trees, herbs, grass	3. One-celled organisms
4. Sun, moon, stars	4. Fish, simple plants
5. Fish, birds, whales	5. Amphibians, reptiles, complex plants (trees, herbs)
6. Cattle, creeping things	6. Mammals, birds, whales, beasts, man

Notice that the sun, moon and stars are created on the fourth day. From an evolutionary point of view, these should be some of the first things produced. Trees and herbs are complex plants and should appear on an evolutionary time scale late. The Genesis record says they appeared earlier, on day three. According to the "Day Age" theory, these same plants would have to wait a "long age" before there was any sunlight (day 4) to grow. They would have to wait even longer for birds (day 5) or creeping things (day 6) to aid in pollination for reproduction. Those birds (day 5) feeding on bugs would also have to wait a long time to feast on their favorite food (day 6).

Now we may twist the meaning of Genesis 1 to "force" agreement with evolution. However, to do so is to change the clear meaning of literal days. If we cannot trust God to mean what He says in the very first book of the Bible, how can we trust Him later, say, in John 3:16 ?

> *"For God so loved the world, that He gave His only begotten Son, that whoever believes in Him should not perish but have everlasting life."*

What Is A Body to Do?

I believe both evolution and creation are matters of faith and outside the ability of science to clearly "prove" either one. The best anyone can do is to try to determine which one makes the most sense. Which one appears to explain the final product, what we do see, the best? Once you have looked at all the facts then decide. Whichever way you choose, do you really have the right to belittle or degrade another's intelligence who chooses differently? I believe in God and that He gave man a choice to believe in Him and accept Him or not. There are highly intelligent people on both sides.

Discussion Points

- Can science prove either evolution or creation? Why or why not?

- Which of the origin models are matters of faith? Explain.

- What does do the laws of thermodynamics tell us about the universe?

- Do compromises between evolution and creation work? Why or why not?

CHAPTER 2 – Life: How Complex is the Problem?

Years ago, when our son was little, he would tell us of some fantastic project he was going to tackle and build. It may have been a vehicle to transport him and his friends around, or an elaborate house. He would gather a few meager materials, what tools he could find, and a few friends to help. His enthusiasm was always incredible! I wish we could have bottled it up. He had the ability to captivate his little friends. One time I asked one of them what they were going to build. He responded with, "I don't know but it is going to be awesome." Invariably, however, the project fell by the wayside and the boys' attention was diverted to something else. You see, they never really thought through or understood the difficulties involved in such projects. They did not know how hard it would be. They did not understand the principles needed to engineer such projects. They had no idea of the tools, time, and materials or whether the project was even possible. They had not really thought it through. The same is also true in building living things. Just how hard is it to produce a simple cell, a multi-cellular organism, or an extraordinarily complex living being such as man? Once we determine the difficulty, then we can examine whether we really have the "tools" to complete the task.

How Hard Can It Be to Create A Simple Cell?

If you take a glass of water from a bubbling stream and hold it up to the light, it may appear clear even drinkable. Take that same water and scrutinize it under a high-powered microscope and you may be astounded at what is in it. The glass of water is far more complex than we may think. The same is also true of the simplest living organism.

In every basic biology textbook, there is a description of the "simple cell". Usually, examples are included with such names as an amoeba or a paramecium with an accompanying illustration such as the following.

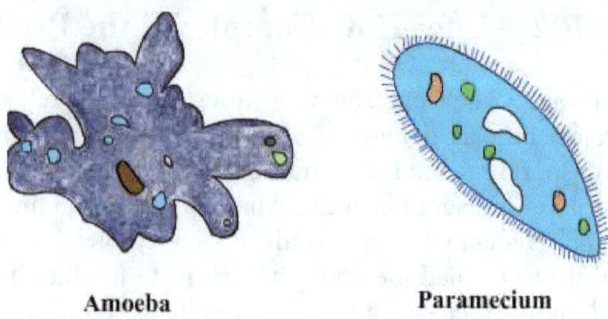

Amoeba   Paramecium

These "simple cells" are not so simple. In fact, they are incredibly complex. Each part of the cell, like the cell membrane, the nucleus, or the interior, is extraordinarily complex by itself as in the following illustration.

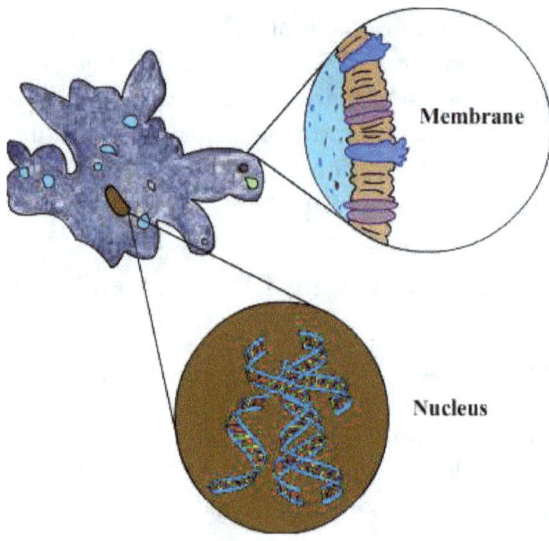

These "simple cells" are like tiny little complex factories and there are many functions that all must work together for the cell to survive and function. These include:

- An outer membrane to hold and protect the cell
- A mechanism to move the cell to a source of raw materials
- A trigger mechanism to open the membrane to good raw materials
- A mechanism to produce energy for the other functions of the cell
- A transport mechanism to move the materials to a decomposition site
- A decomposition site to breakdown the material into useable pieces
- Transportation to move the useable pieces to a construction site

- A construction site to build molecules
- A machine to fold the new constructed molecules
- Transportation to move the molecule to its final resting place
- A mechanism to remove waste
- A central processor to kept track of and control all the functions

Even in the simplest cell there are thousands of different nucleic acids, proteins, and other molecules arranged in complex patterns to handle these functions. All must be present for the cell to function properly and the loss of even one type of molecule may hurt or even kill the cell. If the raw materials cannot enter, the cell starves. If the materials cannot be converted to energy, the cell runs out of gas and dies. If the waste cannot be removed, the cell drowns in its own refuse and so forth. The simple cell is not simple!

The atheist envisions this entire cell came together by chance. If this is true, then random processes produced the individual molecules within the cell and when all were present somehow the cell came to life. Is this possible?

Let's look for a moment at a relatively tiny part of a cell, a protein molecule, and see how difficult it would be to put this molecule together by chance.

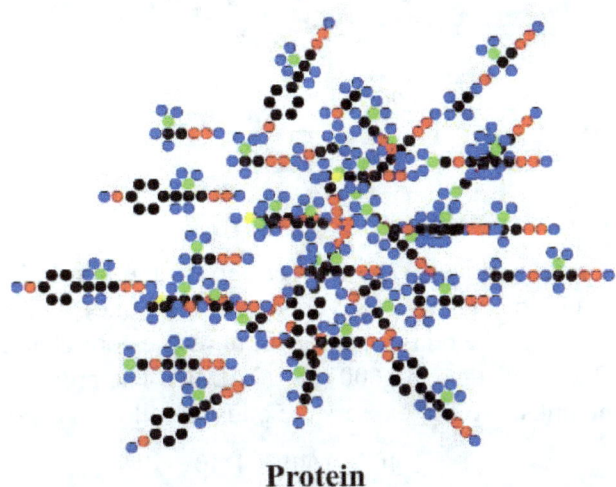

Protein

A simple protein is made up of about 100 links or building blocks called

Because They Said So Isn't Good Enough

amino acids. There are at least 20 different amino acids occurring in nature. Each one, although made from the same elements, can have a structure that is either oriented one way or its mirror image. The structures are referred to as a left-handed or right-handed version. Interestingly in nature, only the left-handed version is ever found in living things. Our simple protein must also have a precise ordering of these left-handed amino acids to be functional within the cell. One amino acid out-of-place and the protein may not be able to do its assigned job or, worse, be harmful to the cell.

To better visualize the problem, imagine a huge bowl with an unlimited supply of amino acids both left-handed and right-handed versions of each one.[6] Now imagine we are going to build our protein link by link. We reach into our bowl and randomly select an amino acid for the first link.

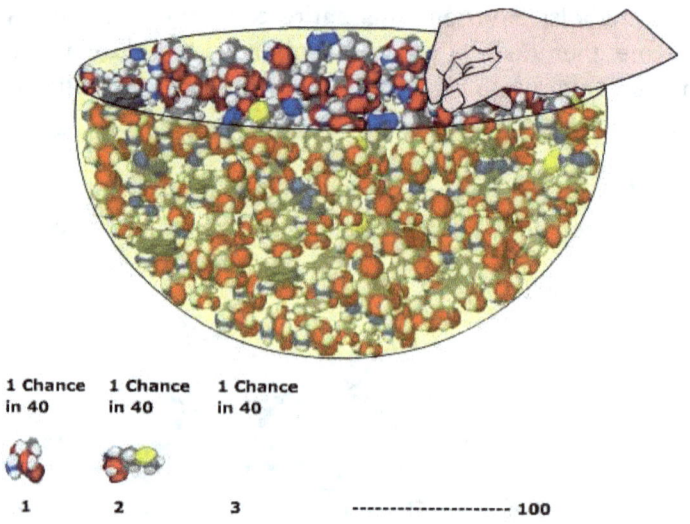

The odds that we will select the correct one for the first link are 1 in 40 (20 different amino acids times 2 versions of each one). The same is true for the second link. The odds that we will draw the correct amino acid for links 1 and 2 are 1 chance in 1600 (1/40 X 1/40). The process is the same for rest of the links. We can express the odds as follows:

$$1/40 \times 1/40 \times 1/40$$
For 100 links or 1 chance in 40^{100}

Expressed as a power of 10 this is 1 chance in 10^{160}.

---

6   *Amino acids can be difficult to produce naturally.*

Just How Big Are These Odds?

Let me use some comparisons to illustrate how enormous the odds are against producing a simple protein by chance. The shading represents the numbers for each illustration as compared to the odds of a protein by chance. In each case the numbers are not even close to the odds.

One Chance In	
Winning the Lottery Answer:	**Estimate of the Total Words in all the Books ever Written Answer:**
1000000000000000000000000000000 0000000000000000000000000000000 0000000000000000000000000000000 0000000000000000000000000000000 0000000000000000000000000000000 000000	1000000000000000000000000000000 0000000000000000000000000000000 0000000000000000000000000000000 0000000000000000000000000000000 0000000000000000000000000000000 000000
Spending 1 Trillion Dollars per second for the assumed age of the earth (~5 billion years) Answer	**Considered impossible by scientists Answer**
1000000000000000000000000000000 0000000000000000000000000000000 0000000000000000000000000000000 0000000000000000000000000000000 0000000000000000000000000000000 000000	1000000000000000000000000000000 0000000000000000000000000000000 0000000000000000000000000000000 0000000000000000000000000000000 0000000000000000000000000000000 000000

"Total Words = 500 (words/page) X 500 (pages/book) X 10,000 (copies) X 10,000,000 (books/year) X 4000 (years)"

These odds, also, are not for the whole organism but only a tiny fraction of the living cell. If the simple protein were like a brick then the entire cell would be like looking at the Pentagon by comparison. Each of the other components of the cell has similar, or even greater odds, and these parts must be present simultaneously if the cell is to emerge as a living cell. A single part missing could prevent these components forming into our "simple cell". The odds against a simple protein emerging by chance are staggering. As unbelievably large as these odds are, however, they pale in comparison to the odds of the entire cell forming by chance. The number gets so large we cannot even represent it. If I typed a one and then zeros in place of each word on every page of this book, I still would not come close to representing the odds against a simple cell being produced by chance! How then could a simple cell ever have just happened? If you believe that it just did, you have far more faith than I do.

There are no stages in between the components and the whole cell. Proteins cannot survive by themselves. In fact, normal environmental pressures such as a little heat or exposure to chemicals can destroy them. The second law of thermodynamics is always at work. It may even be worse for more complex molecules. Unless everything is in place and fully functional, there is no cell. The cell is like a carefully constructed impeccably engineered piece of complex machinery. Can such a thing really be the result of random chance?

From Simple to Complex

Let's assume for the moment that somehow God made the first cell and then chance took over to change this cell over time into all the organisms we see today.

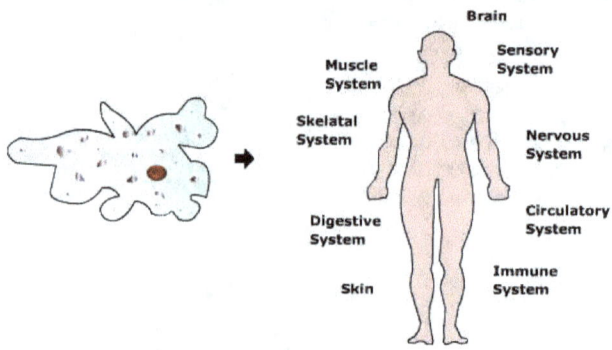

Single Cell To Man

Now the cell must change from a completely self-contained entity to a multi-cell organism with all the cells dependent on each other. Each cell mechanism must evolve from:

- *A simple outer membrane to an outer skin.* The skin is made of multiple cells that is flexible, water resistant, self-healing, self-replenishing and must serve as a protective barrier.

- *A simple source of movement to a complex muscular skeletal system* that is strong, flexible, and completely coordinated.

- *A simple food input system to a complex input, grinding, transport system to the stomach.*

- *A simple decomposition system to a complex digestive and absorption system.*

- *A simple transport system to a complex blood and lymphatic system.*

- *A simple construction system to complex cellular factories* to replace every part of the organism over time.

- *A simple waste removal system to an incredibly complex one.* A liver and kidneys are added to remove waste from the blood and transport it to bulk elimination systems.

- *A simple control system to an extremely complex brain and nervous system.* This brain must now receive evaluate, and respond to sensory systems (eye, ear, taste, smell, and touch). Each of those subsystems are incredible engineered to their tasks. The human brain is often described as the most complex form of matter in the universe.

Besides these changes, there are other systems that must be added to protect the multi-cellular organism. For example:

- *Red blood cells* are added and a lung mechanism to the heart transport system to carry oxygen to every other cell in the body. A simple cell would just get the oxygen it needs from its watery environment.

- *An extremely complex immune system* to protect the whole body from attacks by single cell viruses and bacteria. In a simple cell world, the loss of some simple cells does not affect any of the other cells that have not come under attack. The loss of key cells in a complex body, however, may end up killing the entire body. The immune system fends off such attacks to protect the whole.

The cells in the more complex living things have such an interdependency that they may not be able to survive alone outside the whole body. The red blood cell in your blood, for example, cannot survive on its own. The nerve cell carrying messages through the spinal cord will not survive long outside the body. These specialized cells so vital to the overall functioning of the organism often lose the independent mechanisms that allow the cell to survive on its own. They may lose, for example, their mobility and must now be dependent on other cells and systems to supply their needs. That loss of mobility can be very problematic. They cannot move to a source of food. They cannot go to a source of oxygen. The best they can do is push the waste just outside their membrane, but they cannot take it away. If the cell cannot get food or oxygen or remove waste, the cell dies. Those specialized cells must also have all the mechanisms in place to supply the needs lost due to their new function. They cannot wait for those functions to develop. We now have the same problem of a complete protein waiting for a cell to live in. Just as the protein will not survive without the cell, a cell which has lost independence cannot survive without the whole body. The evolutionist will say that anything is possible given enough time. I believe that all these changes must have occurred in an extremely short period of time otherwise how could the individual parts survive?

Let me use an analogy here to make my point. Higher-level organisms are a little like our more advanced societies. When our country was largely rural, people were more independent. They grew their own food. They made their own clothes. The houses they built often came from the materials they found on their property. All that has now changed. A large percentage of people now live in urban cities and we are extremely dependent on each other, whether we like it or not. If the only food we could eat was what we grew on our own property, we would all starve to death. It is similar for clothes and other material things we have. If you think you are independent, let's see how well you do the next time the power goes off or the water is turned off indefinitely. We did not go from independent to dependent overnight that is true, but we would have no chance of creating our modern society unless there was an incredible spirit of co-operation augmented by careful engineering and planning. Many societies today live the same as they did thousands of years ago. There has been no growth, little development. If they try to live close together without any planning, the result is often a cesspool for squalor, disease, and death. These same areas, though, can be turned into modern, thriving, interdependent societies almost overnight when there is careful intelligent planning, engineering, and execution.

Single cells to complex organisms face much greater obstacles. Some must gain a special ability or job, yet, until the organism is fully developed, the ability may add little value. The red cell, for example, in the blood can load up on oxygen from the lungs, carry it through the blood, and deliver it to other cells. If there are no lung cells yet to supply the oxygen, no blood to carry the red blood cell, and no place to deliver to, of what use is this special ability? A white cell capable of sounding the alarm against a virus entering the body is useless until it is part of a body with an immune system capable of responding to the alarm. What good are brain cells if there is no body to manage and control?

Many functional components within the body must be fully developed or they are useless or, worse, detrimental to the body. The eye, for example, is an absolute marvel but it can only work and be of use when every part of the eye is functional.

The Eye

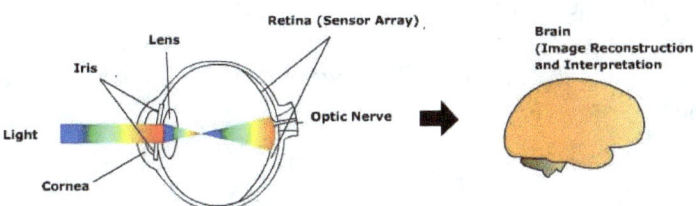

A blind man may have an eye that appears perfectly normal but something in the mechanism just does not work and prevents him from seeing. Perhaps his cornea is clouded. The muscles do not work for proper focusing. The retina has been damaged so that it cannot respond to the incoming light or the optic nerve is not carrying the signals to the brain. You can even have these things working properly and the brain not able to interpret the signals properly. The whole thing must be complete to be functional and therefore useful. A useless eye, however, can be a handicap. Those two useless eyes may be a source of pain (try getting hit there). They are weak areas of the skull through which a hard object could penetrate more easily into the brain and kill.

There are bodily systems as well that must be fully functional or the whole body may not survive. Many of these systems have checks and balances to maintain themselves and prevent going to extremes. Take, for example, the blood stream. There are red cells that carry oxygen from the lungs to every part of the body and remove carbon dioxide waste. Platelets help plug the holes to prevent blood loss when objects penetrate the skin. White cells sound the alarm and combat invading organisms. Even non-cellular liquid portion is vital to the blood system. Besides being the conduit to carry the cells to all parts of the body, it supplies nutrients to other cells. It removes wastes. It helps stimulate proper reactions. It keeps the cells and liquid parts of the body from becoming too acidic or basic which would eventually destroy the body. A failure of any part of the blood system could potentially destroy the whole body. If red cells do not do their job, the body suffocates one cell at a time. No platelets and the body may bleed to death. Failure of one part of the white cell immune functions and the body dies eventually from some opportunistic disease that a healthy immune system would fight off. That is exactly what happens with the disease AIDS.

We could go on and on with one part of the body or subsystem after another. From the tiniest single cell to the most complex living thing, they are all wonders of engineering. How then could any of them ever happen by chance? Consider this, if you found a watch lying on the sand along the edge of the seashore. What would be your first thought as to how it got there.

David P. Mcintyre

I have asked this question many times of a variety of people. No one says that the action of the sea against the sand, the wind, the rain, and sunlight produced the watch. Most of the time people simply assume someone dropped the watch there. If I ask the same question about a rock on the beach, I get an entirely different answer. Why is this? The watch you see exhibits design. It is engineered to be a watch. We can recognize design even if we did not know what it was. The action of the sea, wind, rain and sunlight would never make the watch. In fact, these things would destroy it rather than create it.

Even the simplest living thing is far more complex than the watch. The watch is but a rock in comparison to the simplest cell. If we would never think a watch could possibly be produced by chance, how then can we believe that a living thing infinitely more complex than the watch could be produced that way? I leave this chapter with my favorite quote from Sir Fred Hoyle, at the time, an English astronomer and Professor of Astronomy at Cambridge University:

> *"The chance that higher life forms might have emerged in this way is comparable with the chance that 'a tornado sweeping through a junkyard might assemble a Boeing 747 from the materials therein'"*[7]

---

7   Sir Fred Hoyle. "Hoyle on Evolution" in *Nature*, vol. 294. (1981), p.105.

Discussion Points

- Is the simple cell simple? Explain.

- Do you think that given enough time a cell could be produced by chance? Why or why not?

- If you started with a simple cell, do you think it is possible to evolve by chance to more complex organisms? Explain.

- Can such transition occur without careful planning? Explain.

Chapter 3 – Overcoming the Odds: Does Nature Really have the Tools?

To say that it would be extremely difficult to produce life by chance is undoubtedly the height of understatement. There would have to be incredibly potent mechanisms to overcome such odds. The question for this chapter is *"do these mechanisms exist?"* If they do exist, can they overcome the odds?

There are two basic mechanisms cited to overcome the odds and produce life:

- Mutations
- Natural Selection

We will look at each of these mechanisms but first let me say that I am not arguing against their existence. They do occur in living things. The only question is whether these mechanisms, by themselves or taken together, can overcome the odds and produce evolutionary change.

Mutations

Mutations are often in the news these days. We hear of one virus mutating and producing a new strain of influenza. Another mutates, and we have a new mosquito transmitted disease. A bacterium mutates and there is another new problem for the medical profession. Mutations are everywhere. Certainly, they would have to be the key to overcoming the odds to produce and evolve life. Scientists seem to think so. Hollywood knows so. Have you noticed the number of mutation heroes that have been portrayed on the screen in the last few years? Radiation zaps somebody and now you have the likes of the Incredible Hulk. Another gets bitten by a deadly spider and changes into Spiderman. Even television is starting to get into it. You would think by these superhero stories that getting huge doses of radiation, zapped by lightning, bitten by poisonous insects, drowned in toxic chemicals, and so forth might be a good thing to do. After all, wouldn't it be nice to have the strength of the Hulk or to swing from building to building like Spiderman?

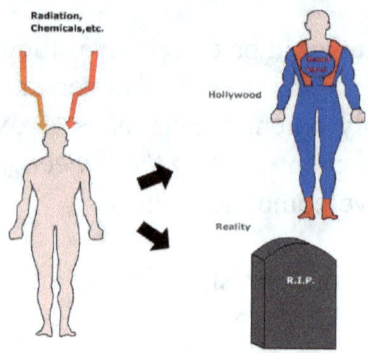

These stories are entertaining, but do they really portray reality? Try asking living survivors of Hiroshima or Nagasaki in World War II, or those that survived Chernobyl whether radiation improved their lives. I doubt you will find anyone that would say it was a good thing and that they have been changed for the better because of it. No, what you will see instead is mutations that hurt, maimed and killed the victims. Those receiving large doses may have died immediately. Others lingered for days, or weeks, or even months and then died agonizing deaths. Still others had their lifespan shortened or their ability to reproduce destroyed. Radiation does not produce superheroes. It kills. It can produce mutations, but most of the mutations are detrimental to the organism not beneficial.

It is no different with chemical or electrical or some other induced mutations. They are virtually all, if not all, harmful to the organism. Cancer cells in the body, for example, are often mutated cells caused by exposure to chemicals. How many of you would think that getting cancer increases your odds of becoming the next link upward in "human evolution"? Even the mutations in bacteria or viruses are not necessarily good for the virus or bacteria. These biological organisms require a host to survive. Mutations that kill the host eventually kill the virus or bacteria. The only good mutation would be one that proved mutually beneficial for both the host and the organism. Even if 10 percent of the mutations were good, how would that help? That is like saying, "I am going to make progress by taking one step forward and then 9 steps back, then another step forward and 9 steps back", and so on. We not only have to overcome the odds against building life by chance but also the odds against getting only good mutations in one organism.

Changes in chromosomes have been observed in many living things including human beings. These are mutations at the genetic level. The question is not whether they occur but rather are they beneficial to the organism. Only beneficial changes can lead to a higher form of life. Harmful ones weaken the organism. I was curious what the medical profession had to say about genetic mutations, so I looked in one of my wife's books. The American Medical Association Encyclopedia of Medicine states:

> *"Carrying a mutant gene can have various effects. In some cases, it affects the structure of the protein whose manufacture the gene directs. Depending on the importance of the protein and the change in its structure, this usually has a disadvantageous effect, ranging from mild to lethal. Moreover, the mutant gene may be passed on to some of the person's own children. Diseases or disorders that result from such mutant genes are known as genetic disorders. Very rarely, genetic mutations occur that have a positively beneficial effect."*[8]

I do not know what the percentage of good mutations would be as compared to bad ones, but I think most are usually bad. We might get a clue, however, by looking at the list of genetic disorders versus the list of positively beneficial effects. The same encyclopedia goes on to categorize diseases into abnormal number of chromosomes, single defective gene diseases and multi-defective gene diseases. Without belaboring which category each fall into, here is a partial list:

---

[8] Charles B. Clayman, MD, Medical Editor. *The American Medical Association Encyclopedia of Medicine* (New York: Random House, 1989), p. 479.

Down's Syndrome
Huntington's chorea
Neurofibromatosis
Tuberous sclerosis
Albinism
Cystic fibrosis
Fredrich's ataxia
Sickle Cell Anemia
Tay-Sachs disease
Color blindness
Fragile X syndrome
Hemophilia
Muscular dystrophy
Diabetes mellitus

I only listed the ones I have heard about. There were others in the encyclopedia that I did not recognize and even the lists presented were referred to as examples. Other diseases, such as heart disease, may also have genetic links.

I looked up in the same book examples of beneficial mutations. The only one listed was the mutation that causes the sickle cell trait. Apparently, this mutation protects against malaria.[9] Interestingly, sickle cell anemia is described in another place in the book as "… a chronic very severe form of anemia (reduced oxygen-carrying capacity of the blood)".[10] The description alone does not sound good for the person with this trait. I can well understand why the malaria parasite might not do well in a person with reduced oxygen-carrying capacity. In fact, the person with such a trait may not do very well. If you think that this mutation is really a beneficial one, just ask yourself would you like to have the sickle cell trait so that you can be protected against getting malaria?

---

9   Clayman, p.708.
10   Clayman, p. 904

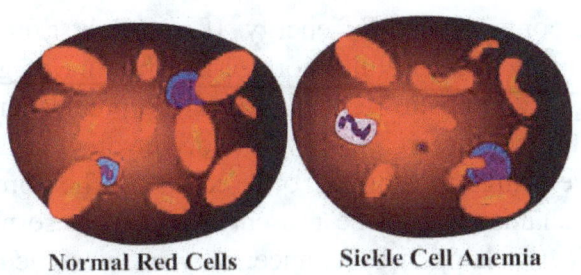

Normal Red Cells   Sickle Cell Anemia

That Pesky 2nd Law Again

Remember the 2nd law of thermodynamics I talked about earlier? It is precisely at the genetic and molecular level where we consistently see it operating. If left alone, reactions do not tend toward a more ordered state but a more disordered state. We start out at a higher level and a change occurs that lowers the level. However, during the downward trend, we see in nature what appears to be an increase in order. Babies are born and grow up to adults. Plants grow from a seed. Certain parts of the body may heal itself or grow a new part. These examples, as well as others, have been used as proof that it is possible to become more ordered. The argument is that while the whole universe may be running down, certain parts may be building up. We use up energy, say from the sun, that in turn allows upward evolution to occur on the earth. We use up energy from undersea volcanic activity that spawns new life around the volcano. But is this true?

There is a huge flaw in the whole concept. Energy by itself does not improve things. You can have an unlimited supply of energy and things will likely get worse and worse. Think of all the major storms that you may have heard about. For example, Hurricanes: Andrew, Wilma, and Irma, that came through Florida packed an incredible punch. Periodically, we hear of other storms and their effects. The news speaks of devastation not creation. Living things in an energy storm fair no better than objects. The same news often speaks of deaths. On a molecular level, huge amounts of energy can be even more destructive. No, the only ways to improve something is to very carefully control and direct the energy. A tank of gasoline contains a lot of energy. If you light a match to it, it will blow up. If you carefully control the mixture of gasoline and air entering a combustion chamber and the precise timing of the lighting of the mixture, it allows you to drive your car. Energy alone cannot drive things to a higher ordered state. The controlling and guiding mechanisms must be present as well. These mechanisms, however, do not happen by chance; they are designed. Have you ever seen a tornado, a tidal wave, or a hurricane produce a car? I have purchased a vehicle from a company with many intelligent engineers that designed my car.

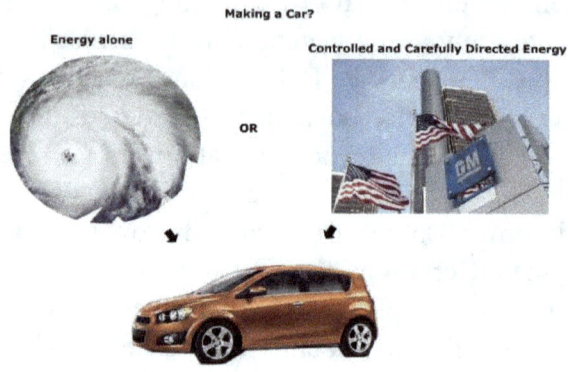

Living things are far more complex than even the most complex engine. The controlling and directing mechanisms are extremely complex. We understand a car engine well, yet we have trouble completely understanding the mechanisms in living things. What we do know is that only as these mechanisms function properly does the baby grow up or the seed become a tree. Even if they both reach maturity, if the controlling mechanisms begin to fail, the adult begins to deteriorate. Do you think you can do the same things at 50 years old that you did at 15? The controlling and directing mechanisms are the only things that for a time can hold back the downward trend of that pesky 2nd law. If these mechanisms are missing, upward evolution is impossible. If they fail, the downward spiral is immediate. Consider how long it takes after an animal dies that it becomes pretty rank. These mechanisms are so complex; how could they possibly happen by chance?

But Couldn't Small Changes Lead to Big Changes?

You can believe that small changes over time will eventually lead to big positive changes if you wish. That is not what we generally observe. Those small dings on your car do not improve the car and neither do small changes improve the organism. The 2nd law is potent on small changes. They hurt the organism. Consider this, would you beat on a black and white TV and expect that over time it will eventually change into a HD color TV?

That is in simplistic terms what we are expecting to happen with living things. The outside forces that generate change, heat, electricity, radiation, chemicals and so forth, "beat" on the organism. Most of these forces eventually result in death. A small number may be incorporated into the genetic code and therefore have the potential of being passed on to the offspring. These changes, however, are virtually always harmful.

Single cell organisms with changed genetic code invariably produce organisms that are defective and less able to survive. DNA itself often weeds out the changes with an error correcting mechanism. Scientists studying the genetic code are intrigued by the DNA's ability to fix itself in many cases. It is precisely this kind of ability that is leading researchers to explore the possibility of correcting certain genetic problems such as diabetes by "fixing" the flawed genetic code. These fixes, however, just bring the genetic code back to the original code for the organism. It does not change the organism into something new. Small changes that might lead to something beneficial may also be "corrected" thus increasing the odds against small changes leading to big positive changes.

> Does this DNA error correcting mechanism sound like the work of blind chance or an incredibly intelligent master designer?

Given Enough Time, Isn't Anything Possible?

Many have thought that if there is enough time and enough chemical interaction that the needed controlling molecules and mechanisms would eventually appear. The typical argument is often illustrated by suggesting that monkeys banging on typewriters long enough will eventually type out the works of Shakespeare or some other great work. Does this argument really make sense?

As hard as we may try, we cannot get away from that 2nd law. If we are to make the monkey illustration realistic, the typewriter keys must fail, the paper deteriorate, the ink erase from the paper and so forth. That is the 2nd law in action. Thus, after 1,000 years of typing, the monkeys are no further along than when they started. Millions or billions of years will not make any difference. In fact, according to the 2nd law, the monkeys would probably be extinct before the first line is completed. Those of you that believe this is possible (and you have that right), are you really acting from knowledge or faith?

Natural Selection

Natural Selection, "Survival of the Fittest", appears in all the biology textbooks. It is one of the most important referenced mechanisms supposedly evolving every species. I am not saying it does not occur. It does. The only question is whether this observed mechanism enhances a species.

Natural selection does not create anything new. All the competing organisms must already exist. Even the weakest organisms survive when there is no competition. It is only when there are stronger organisms that the weak are weeded out over time. The real source of organisms with an edge over the others must come from the other mechanisms such as mutations. As we have already discussed, most of these (maybe even all) are harmful to the organism. Natural selection would tend to kill those mutant organisms off over time. Animals or humans, for example, with mutant genes leaving them susceptible to disease would eventually be unable to compete with their less disease prone counterparts. Natural selection would weed them out. One mechanism (mutations) negates the other. If anything, natural selection would maintain status quo.

Let us suppose for the sake of the argument that a mutation occurs which appears to be leading toward an advantage for the organism. Notice I said, "leading toward an advantage". Unless the mutation produces a completely formed and useful advantage, it could be a hindrance not some help to the organism. Suppose a fish sticks his head above water and notices the nice green things on land. If only he could get to them and eat them. One day he sprouts in place of a fin the beginnings of a leg. Now the leg is not fully formed so it cannot support his weight. It is too bad he cannot get up to those green things today. He swims off but curiously begins swimming in a circle, as the newly formed leg cannot keep up with the normal fin on the other side. Suddenly he spots his mortal enemy a bigger fish ready to eat him. He frantically tries to swim away only to find himself totally out of control. The bigger fish easily pounces and has him for lunch. Even if the leg were fully formed, it still would not help. With only one leg he is a cripple on land and an easy prey in the water. Even if he developed two legs and he could get to the green stuff on land, he would die from suffocation because he has not yet developed lungs to survive on land. If he develops lungs first, he might have a disadvantage as a small fish because now he would periodically have to come up for air. The surface of the water is much more precarious than being able to hide on the bottom.

Fish to Amphibian

This same scene could be played out with other transitions as well. Consider a lizard hoping to gain an advantage over his enemies by escaping to the sky.

Reptile To Bird

One day he sprouts a few feathers on one leg. Now he is even worse off because the feathers keep hanging up on the undergrowth as he runs. He is now easier pray for his enemies. Later another lizard pops out a fully formed wing. Then that big old bully comes around. He tries to flap that one wing but to no avail because with only one wing he cannot fly. He tries to run away but now cannot move as fast because a wing does not make a good leg. He is desperate. Frantically he tries to escape. He might have made it to his hiding place with two good legs but not now. Natural selection hinders progress again. Another lizard pops out two wings and is ready to fly to freedom but realizes too late he does not have the proper muscles and movement to make the wings work properly Finally, another lizard pops out of the egg with fully developed wings but lacks the other appendages needed to feed himself or move properly when on the ground. He dies of starvation or is eaten because he is too weak to fly. The whole thing must be fully functional and integrated into the organism to be useful. Meanwhile our predator is just hoping another change will occur, so he can scarf up another easy meal.

You see, unless things are fully developed, they may not be advantages but hindrances to the organism. To produce fully developed items requires a huge number of simultaneous good mutations, all integrated with each other.

> Which is easier to believe that nature was extremely lucky or that a master designer designed each organism?

Certainly, some animals are better equipped than others to win out in competition or direct confrontation (such as predator and prey) with others. Curiously, those species on the bottom of the food chain often produce incredible numbers of offspring while those at the top produce very few. Consider the shrimp and the shark or the rabbit and the lion. It is almost as if someone wants to level the playing field so that all species have a chance to survive.

Discussion Points

- Would mutations and natural selection lead to a more evolved form of life? Explain.

- Do you think that given enough time anything is possible? Why or why not?

- Can a partially developed new addition to the organism (ex. eye, ear, etc.) or a partially converted existing appendage (ex. fin to a leg, leg to a wing, etc.) improve the organism's chance of survival? Why or why not?

CHAPTER 4 – Aren't There Proofs That Evolution is True?

There was a big story awhile back about the Martian meteorite that landed in Antarctica and, supposedly, contained evidence of life. The story made the front pages of many newspapers. The rock was said to be formed on Mars 3.6-4 billion years ago and blasted away from the planet about 16 million years ago. It then floated in space for millions of years and finally came to earth about 13,000 years ago[11]. It was heralded as the first breakthrough evidence that life exists in outer space. But was it?

Before we talk about evidence, I think it is important that we talk about ground rules for presenting evidence. I have listed below the basic rules I believe should be followed:

- Present all the evidence.
- Always separate fact from interpretation.
- Never falsify evidence.
- Do not discard alternate explanations for the evidence because of personal beliefs.

Do these seem like common sense? I believe they are. Somehow, when our beliefs are so strong (remember we are really talking about beliefs here), we seem to throw out common sense. Let me take each rule in turn to make the point.

Present All the Evidence

If we fail to present all the evidence, we can come to the wrong conclusions. In a court of law, the object is to present all the evidence so that the jury can make an informed decision about the guilt or innocence of the defendant. Have you ever watched a courtroom drama on TV? In many of them, it appears as if one person is guilty through most of the program until a crucial piece of evidence is presented. The picture then becomes clear and the real guilty party is uncovered. In real life, many prisoners have been proven innocent or guilty by newer information such as DNA testing. All evidence should be presented and when it is, we come to a better conclusion. Often bias tends to make us either cover up or ignore evidence.

---

11 Allan Hills 84001 , Wikipedia

In the meteorite story, the facts were that a meteorite was found in Antarctica and that it contained some curious spicules. It also had a certain chemical composition that resembled chemical composition of rocks analyzed by a Mars probe.

This leads me to the next rule.

Always Separate Fact from Interpretation

The facts were that the rock was found in Antarctica with the characteristics I just stated. The interpretation was that it came from Mars. I think most reasonably intelligent people could have asked a few simple cross-examining questions to ascertain the truth. Imagine the person announcing the discovery is sitting on the witness stand. You approach and begin your cross-examination.

Question: When was the rock found?
Witness: In 1984.

Question: When was it determined that it came from Mars?
Witness: In 1993.

Question: How long ago did it come from Mars?
Witness: We believe that it left Mars some 16 million years ago and then crashed on earth about 13,000 years ago.

Question: Was there any documented evidence, eyewitness reports, or other direct evidence that it came from Mars?
Witness: No.

Question: How do you know for certain that it came from Mars?
Witness: It contains similar chemical makeup of rocks found on Mars.

Question: Have you tested samples from all the other planets, moons, and so forth in the Solar system to rule out the possibility that it came from somewhere else?
Witness: Well, no.

Question: Then it could have come from somewhere else?
Witness: Well, possibly, but we believe it came from Mars.

Question: What was in the rock that made you think it contained evidence of life?
Witness: Wormlike objects.

Question: Were these actual worms?
Witness: No, they were crystalline spicules.

Question: Could they have been produced by other means?
Witness: Well, yes.

Question: Like how?
Witness: Weathering of mineral grains could produce similar structures.

Question: Have such structures been seen from meteorites from other places?
Witness: Yes, from the moon.

Question: Is it not true that life does not and cannot exist on the moon?
Witness: Yes.

Question: Do all scientists agree with the reported conclusions?
Witness: Well, no.

Question: Since recorded history is only about 6000 years old and modern science is less than 500 years old, how can you be so certain that all this happened in the time frames reported?
Witness: It fits with our present scientific theories of origins.

Question: And these scientific theories are based on what?
Witness: The theory of evolution.

We could continue this for quite a while, but I think you get my point. The facts are that the rock was found with curious worm-like spicules and that it had the characteristics of a meteorite. All the rest is really interpretation. Interpretation is not fact. Interpretation will be based on preconceived ideas on what is true or false, in this case the belief in evolution. It is OK to interpret facts. It is wrong to present interpretations as facts. It is equally wrong to exclude other interpretations. It is interesting that the original announcement of the "Mars rocks" discovery made the front page of newspapers but the later articles attacking or refuting the interpretation did not make the front page.

Which brings me to my next point.

Never Falsify Evidence

I do not think we need to discuss much about this; it is simply wrong to create evidence to try to "prove" preconceived ideas of truth. Science is supposed to correct or adjust itself as new evidence is presented. That is how science is supposed to work (remember the scientific method). Scientists should admit that their theories are wrong when new evidence seems to indicate it. I will admit that giving up those long-time theories is very hard to do. They are like those "blankies" we used to have when we were young children. There may come a time, though, when they must go if we are to make progress. In any case, we should never invent things to justify keeping an old theory.

Let's conclude with my last rule.

Do Not Discard Alternate Explanations for The Evidence Because Of Personal Beliefs

It is OK to have personal beliefs. That is part of who you are. It is simply wrong to discount the beliefs of others when there are no established facts to prove one belief true over another. Remember, no human witnesses were there when all this "evolving" or "creating" was going on. Therefore, there are no established facts only interpretations of the present world we see. Let all interpretations be heard and then let the listeners decide for themselves what makes sense. To do any less, I believe, is simply indoctrination and not in keeping with the principles of science.

With these principles in mind, let us look at some of the evidence.

Vestigial Structures

Examples:

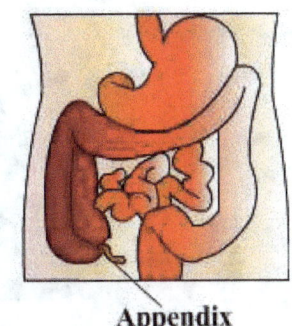

Coccyx - Tail Bone **Appendix**

Vestigial structures are parts of an organism that do not appear to have any function or use. The conclusion is drawn that they must be left over from a previous evolutionary stage. Some texts have cited the tailbone or the appendix in the human body as examples of such structures. Just because we do not know the use of the part, does not mean that the part does not have a use.

Years ago, I noticed a piece of metal sticking out from the top of my outboard motor with a big hole in it. It did not appear to have any function. It had no part in the starting, running, or shifting of the motor. It did not hold anything in place. It was not connected to anything else but the power head. It was just an ugly piece of metal sticking out from the back of the head. One day my power head gave out and had to be rebuilt. That day, I learned the use of this piece of metal while observing the mechanic repair my outboard. He loosened several bolts holding the power head to the lower unit and then proceeded to attach a hook and winch through the hole in the metal. When he tightened the winch the power head separated nicely from the lower unit. You see, the metal piece had a use. The manufacturer of the outboard had added this piece to make it easier to remove and work on the power head.

Because They Said So Isn't Good Enough

Many companies add components, tools, and even spare parts to their products. These items may not be used every day but come in very handy under certain circumstances. The spare tire in the car trunk does not appear to have any use when driving the car. It just takes up space. Is the spare tire a holdover from a previous existence as a three or five-wheel vehicle? I think the answer to that question becomes obvious when you are broken down on the side of the road with a flat tire.

You see, just because we do not know the function of some components of an organism does not mean that it does not have a use. Wouldn't an all-wise creator have produced some parts to aid the organism during certain stages of its life, when threatened, or when hurt? At the turn of the 20th century, there were over 100 so-called vestigial parts that scientists pointed to in the human body including the coccyx and the appendix. Over the years, most of these parts are now known to have a purpose. You would have trouble sitting properly without that coccyx bone. The appendix has been found to store bacteria needed by the gut for proper digestion. Scientists would be better off saying, "We do not know the purpose of certain components in an organism," rather than ascribing them to holdovers from a previous evolutionary existence. Such conclusions do not separate the facts from the interpretation and totally ignore alternative explanations.

David P. Mcintyre

Embryonic Recapitulation

This concept is based on the idea that the fetus in the womb goes through all the previous evolutionary stages on its way to becoming a human being. At different stages it resembles a fish, an amphibian, a mammal, and so forth. It was first presented in the late 1800's by the German biologist Ernst Haeckel and was referred to by the slogan "ontogeny recapitulates phylogeny". Is this true?

First, the drawings were fabricated to make it appear as though the growth stages "recapitulated" the evolutionary stages, a clear violation of the rule to never falsify evidence.

Secondly, even if there were the appearance of similarity it still does not prove actual progression through previous supposed evolutionary stages. The organism may simply be under construction. Suppose you are driving by a house that is under construction on a neighboring street. At first, you notice the land being cleared much like an animal making a nest in the grass. Next, you notice concrete being poured into a wooden structure. The house is now in the stage of a beaver building packing mud into its wooden edifice. Later, you see the walls emerge much like the walls of Stone Hinge. Next comes the roof structure and now it has the appearance of a small gothic cathedral. Finally, the outside walls and roof are finished, and it begins to look more like a house. Has the house really gone through evolutionary stages from a grass clearing, to a beaver structure, to a Stone Hinge, to a gothic cathedral, and then finally to a house? Or has it always been a house in various stages of development? If you had asked the builder, he would have told you that he was simply following the plans he had. At no time was the structure anything but a house. It was simply under construction.

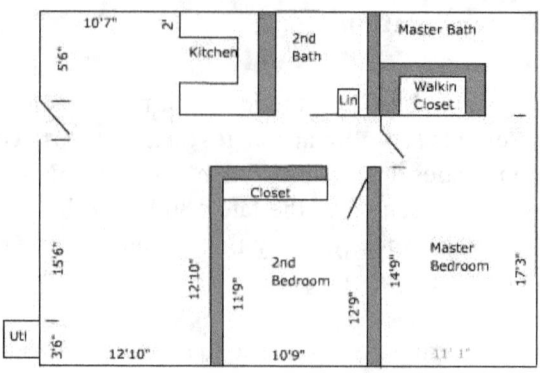

The same concept is true in biology. We know now that every living thing has a blueprint. It is the DNA molecule in the nucleus of the cells. If you could read it you would have a clear description of the final biological product. This blueprint does not change during the development of the organism. Are the changes we observe in the fetus really recapitulation of previous evolutionary existences or are they just changes in a baby under construction? For that matter, what is the difference between the fetus inside the womb undergoing growth and development and the continued growth and development of the baby after birth outside the womb? The DNA has not changed, and it takes years to fully make an adult.

> *"I will praise You, for I am fearfully and wonderfully made; marvelous are Your works, and that my soul knows very well. My frame was not hidden from You, when I was made in secret, and skillfully wrought in the lowest parts of the earth. Your eyes saw my substance, being yet unformed. And in Your book, they were written, the days fashioned for me, when as yet there were none of them."* (Psalm 139:14-16)

Many scientists, especially those who have studied the developing fetus the most, have concluded that Haeckel was totally wrong. Dr. Henry Morris had this to say on the subject:

> *"Modern studies in molecular genetics have shown the impossibility of such concepts. The DNA for a man is not the DNA for a fish, nor is it the DNA for a fish with something added. The DNA for each kind is uniquely programmed to produce its own kind, not to produce a temporary replica of some other kind. Furthermore, embryologic studies have shown that there are so*

many omissions, additions, and inversions in the embryologic sequences, as compared to the supposed evolutionary sequences, that the idea of recapitulation could certainly not be called a law! Even the few apparent parallels are quite superficial and in no sense could represent an actual recapitulation." [12]

Similar Structures

Many textbooks claim that living things with similar looking parts either descended from one another or had a common ancestry. These similarities are presented as proof positive that evolution has occurred but is this true? Could the similarities be intentional? What if these similar structures are merely the application of a design to meet a specific need to different organisms with that need.

Let me use a non-living example to make the point. If someone were to observe all the different internal combustion engines, they might conclude that random chance produced the fuel injection first in the small lawn mower engine. Then, gradually over time these small engines evolved to the larger engines. It might also be concluded that because of the "similarities" in the fuel injection system in outboards and car engines that they had a common ancestor. Those engines with carburetors had a different ancestor. That might be one way to look at the data. There is another way, though. All internal combustion engines have a need to supply fuel to the cylinder. Without the fuel the engine does not run. An engineer develops a more efficient method of injecting small, controlled amounts of fuel to the cylinder at the precise moment the engine needs it. Now the engine runs more smoothly with greater fuel efficiency. We see this design showing up in all kinds of engines from cars to trucks to outboards to almost any internal combustion engine. Is this structure then the result of random chance or purposeful design? Are the differences between the engines (e.g. size of the injection ports, special mechanisms, etc.) the result of evolution or adaptation of a good idea to the special needs of the various types of engines?

---

12   Morris, *Scientific Creationism*, p. 77.

Fuel Injection

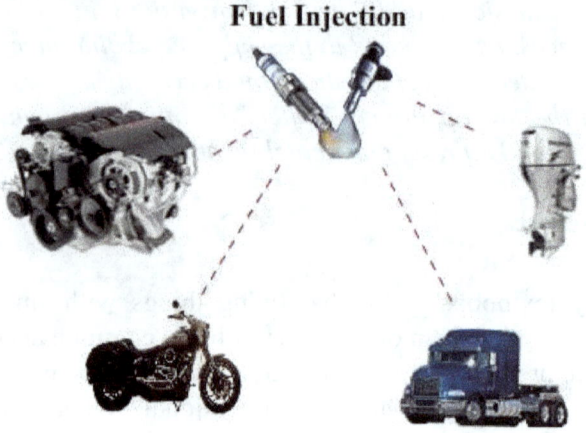

Similar structures could just as easily be cited as proof of a master designer rather than common ancestry. In fact, if an organism is better adapted to its environment, isn't it more likely that the adaptation was put there on purpose? A monkey and a human arm may have similar structure. The monkey's arm is proportionately longer and hands much more adaptable to hanging and swinging from the trees where he lives. The human arm and hands are better for intricate design work.

We must always be on guard and separate the facts from the interpretations of the facts. The facts are that there are similar structures in living things. Different birds may have similar looking legs, wings, and other structures. Four-footed animals may have similar limb structures. The legs on an iguana are better suited for climbing and digging then the legs on a deer. His legs are better adapted to his environment where he must run and jump over things to escape his enemies. We even see similar structures on dissimilar species. There are wings on a bat, a bug, and a bird. If you choose to believe living things evolved, then you will interpret the facts consistent with that assumption. Similar structures could also be indicative of a master engineer who has designed a structure for a specific function. Those living things requiring that function might have a similar looking structure. Did the bug evolve into the bird and then into a bat or did a master designer give each of them specially designed wings because all three would need to be able to fly? The evolutionist must ascribe such similar structures found in unrelated species by a new term: "convergent evolution". Such terminology exhibits bias. In this case, to make it appear as though evolution predicts such structures. I do not agree. I believe that a much better explanation is that a master designer reused a good design for a specific function needed by many species. He incorporated that design into the blueprint for those species.

For some animals, it is ridiculously hard to imagine how they might have evolved. Consider the webfeet of a duckbill platypus, a mammal, and the common duck. How many of you, think the platypus evolved from the duck or vice versa? Both animals do spend a good deal of time in the water where webfeet certainly help. In fact, I think it is such a good idea that I have even put some on my feet every time I go snorkeling. It really helps.

Atavistic Structures

In rare cases, some unnatural structures may appear in the offspring of a species. These may include extra appendages, growths in certain areas (normal parts appearing in abnormal locations), and so forth. The evolutionist interprets these structures to be throwbacks to a previous evolutionary state. Couldn't these also just be mistakes? In the typing of this book, I made many spelling errors (thank God for Spell Check). Was this a throwback to a previous existence or did I just hit the wrong keys? When we consider the incredible complexity of the DNA molecule and the ability of a sperm DNA and an egg DNA to combine into new DNA, does it really seem so farfetched that occasionally there may be an error in the offspring blueprint? In fact, with all the chemical, radiation, contamination and other influences on the process, why are there not more of these structures? Atavistic (throwback) structures are not facts. The name is simply an interpretation of abnormalities that are occasionally seen in living things. Isn't the idea that these structures are mistakes just as good an interpretation (maybe even better)?

The Pepper Moth

The pepper moth has been touted for years as positive proof of evolution. It appears in many if not all the evolution textbooks. There are two types of these moths, one dark-colored and the other light. In England before the industrial revolution, the lighter variety prevailed. They could more easily conceal themselves against the lighter building walls of that time. The darker variety stood out and therefore tended to be seen and eaten more readily. Later, after the industrial revolution, the soot from factories darkened more of the walls. The darker variety now had the advantage and the lighter variety was more easily seen. The population shifted in favor of the darker variety. Evolutionists jumped on this change as absolute proof that evolution has occurred. Is that true, however? What did nature start with before the industrial revolution? The answer is pepper moths. What did they end up with after the industrial revolution? The answer is pepper moths. As I indicated in an earlier chapter, we need to see a change to a higher, more ordered state to prove evolution is true. Both types of pepper moths are the same level. Could we not also argue that a master designer planned the differences in the types to ensure the continuation of pepper moths under a variety of circumstances? If the buildings are cleaned up and the lighter population now prevails again, does this mean that the pepper moths have devolved?

Which brings me to another concept.

Adaptation

Much ado has been made about some species' ability to adapt to different environment conditions. Man has shown great ability to survive in a variety of climates, altitudes, land conditions and available food sources. The question is, "Is adaptation really evidence for evolution or is it the result of careful planning?". If it is the latter, then adaptation is proof of intelligent design.

Consider for a moment an example of intelligent design, the modern jet airliner. It has many items built into the plane that have nothing to do with keeping the plane flying but all important to the survival of the plane and/or its passengers. Extra extensions on the wing help the plane become air-born but may not be needed while the plane is in flight. The number and power of the engines is far more than what is needed for actual flight (many 4 engine planes can fly on just 2 engines). The extra power is just what is needed to become air-born under heavy loads. There are more wheels than are really needed to carry the weight of the plane, but the extra wheels are exactly what would be needed to ensure safety when fully loaded. There are built in tire pressure sensors and, in some, inflating devices. We might say, then, the plane can adapt to various payloads that it might carry. Just before takeoff, the flight attendants apprise you of all the safety features on the plane. There are flotation devices under your seat in case of a water landing. There are oxygen masks in case the cabin suddenly depressurizes. There are special lights to guide you to exits. There are slides to help you exit the plane in a hurry. In addition to safety features, there are lights to be turned on when it is dark, food service to feed hungry passengers on longer flights, individual climate controls, movies to entertain, and more. There are special navigation and communication devices. None of these things are necessary for the plane to fly but all allow the plane to adapt to varying conditions during the flight. These things are not the product of blind chance. Many highly intelligent engineers worked hard to develop and implement them.

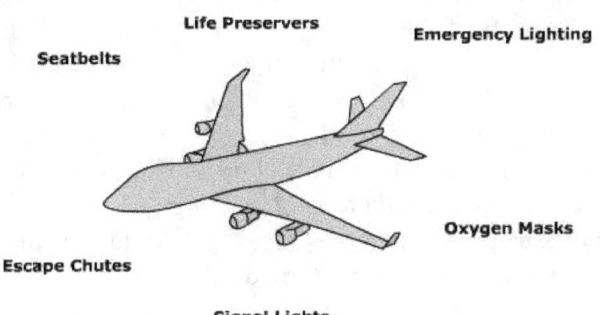

Most of those features in the plane, except for seat belts, are not really used during routine flights. They only become important under special conditions. You do not use the flotation devices until there is a water landing. You do not use the chutes for normal disembarkation from the plane. The oxygen masks do not deploy until the cabin pressure suddenly drops. Certain instruments only become important when visibility is extremely limited. If intelligence is behind the creation of living things, would we not also see such backup and adaptability mechanisms in them as well?

There are many such devices in every one of us. If it gets too hot, we have sweat glands that open to secrete moisture which then evaporates to cool the body down. If it gets too cold, the pores close and we get "goose bumps" which help circulation to warm us up. If we travel to higher altitudes, more red blood cells are produced to ensure an adequate supply of oxygen to the cells in our body. If there is blockage to the flow of blood, alternate pathways are immediately available. Our immune system is continuously alert to invading organisms and responds accordingly. The response is often very targeted. Specific antibodies against the invading organism may be produced to destroy the invader. This response does not have to be learned. Our system is ready to respond even when the organism has never been seen before. There are mechanisms to patch us up when we are cut, to store and retrieve food supplies, and vary the amount of certain needed molecules such as insulin. We could go on and on, but I think you get the point. Are these really the result of random chance or is a master designer at work building in mechanisms to ensure the survival of humans?

Now if you believe that these mechanisms could have developed by chance, then you have an incredible amount of faith. Many of these mechanisms must be fully formed to work properly. If they are only partially formed, they could be detrimental to the body. Consider the sweat gland. It must be able to open when the body is hot and secrete moisture and then close when the body cools. If there is moisture in the skin but no pores to let it out, the moisture may heat up and hurt the body. If the pores open without any moisture, there is no cooling and the pores are open to potential invasions by bacteria or viruses that could hurt the body. If the water mechanism is unable to be turned off, the body dehydrates. If the pores cannot close after being opened, again, the body is susceptible to foreign particle or chemical invasions. The whole process must work, or it may handicap us.

Many processes have complex feedback mechanisms to ensure the response is enough but not too much. The mechanism that produces the extra red blood cells when the oxygen level is low must also have a mechanism that stops production when there are enough cells or even reduce the numbers when oxygen levels increase. Extra cells in the blood passageways are also potential particles to block those same passageways. These extra cells could be the cause of a heart attack or a stroke. If you are cut, triggering a response to patch you up, there must also be a mechanism to stop the clotting. Otherwise, you will die of one big clot. If there is no shutdown mechanism in an antibody response to a bacteria invasion, the antibodies start attacking you. You will swell up like a giant pimple! The whole mechanism must be in place or it can be harmful to the body.

Many diseases such as diabetes, allergies, and arthritis are the result of mechanisms that are not functioning properly. They make the body less able to compete, so how could they have evolved? Isn't it a better explanation that these mechanisms were designed and those that do not work properly are the result of mutations to the original design?

Which brings me to the following.

Fly Mutations

Over the years there have been many experiments on flies to create mutations. The hope is that the mutations will provide proof for evolution and shed light on its mechanisms. The result has been flies mutating to produce extra wings, extra legs, or extra eyes. Many of the flies simply died because of the exposure to a mutagenic agent such as radiation or chemicals. At no time did any of the flies become anything else but flies. The flies with extra wings could no longer fly. Those with extra legs could no longer walk properly. If they had extra eyes, they could not see properly. In all cases, the mutated flies were handicapped and less able to survive. In fact, the only reason they did survive for a time was because the scientists conducting the experiments protected them. If they mutated in the wild, they would have been destroyed (remember "survival of the fittest"). Why then are fly mutations held up as examples of evolution? Are these not just mutations from an original good design from a master designer?

Bombarding flies with radiation or chemicals in the hope of generating insights into evolution is a little like throwing a cat in a hot dryer and or setting dynamite sticks off in a lake. Do you really think things will improve? The same is true of all the efforts to initiate changes in flies through mutagenic agents.

Hybrids

Hybrids are sometimes cited as evidence for evolution. These are the results of crossbreeding of two different animals or plants. One common example is the mule. It is the result of breeding a male donkey with a female horse. Since the mule is sure-footed and strong, supposedly it combines the best of both the donkey and the horse and is therefore more evolved.

Some, however, may argue that conclusion when the famous mule stubbornness is factored in. All kidding aside, does this case really prove evolution? The mule is sterile and therefore cannot reproduce itself. How then can this "new" evolved life survive? There is another explanation. Throughout plant and animal life, there appears to be limits to the ability of life to interbreed. Dogs can interbreed with dogs and cats with cats but not dogs with cats. When we push the limits sterility, deformity, or no life at all results. These boundaries are prevalent throughout nature, from the simplest organisms to the more complex. They are precisely what we would expect if there were a supreme intelligence that wished to provide some evidence for his existence. Let me explain. If every form of life is potentially able to interbreed with everything else, you could make a rather good case that the essence of life is all the same and that life did in fact evolve. But if life is full of isolated islands of complexity where only life within that group can interbreed, then how do you evolve? Mutations, as we have seen, do not help. Interbreeding does not provide a means to escape the group. In fact, special breeding may bring out some bad traits. Certain dog types were bred to produce certain characteristics. The dachshunds, for example, were bred to be able to dig down and enter holes in the ground to get pesky animals that plague farmers. They certainly can do that, but the breed also is known for chronic back problems. Other breeds may be prone to certain diseases, weaknesses in certain body parts, or exhibit emotional or apparent psychological problems. The more we try to breed out of a group or crossbreed to another, the more problems seem to show up. Problems such as these are harmful to the animal and may handicap it in the survival race.

It would take massive changes to produce an animal capable of interbreeding with another group. These changes would have to occur all at once. Small incremental changes, as we have already discussed, may not help at all in moving the animal to a different level and may be detrimental. How do we get that lucky that often to move the evolution of living things ever onward and upward? Isn't it more likely that it was planned that way? A group of engineers in a company may design components for their products in such a way that they may be compatible with other products within the company. Microsoft™ designs its software so that Microsoft Office programs will work well with each other within Windows, but these same products may not work well with products from another company's software. It is planned that way. A car manufacturer may produce a line of cars with some interchangeable parts. These same parts may not fit another manufacturer's cars. Again, it is planned that way by intelligent engineers to make the products unique. These unique designs are logos for the company. Sometimes even the sounds are identified with a specific company. I can almost always tell when a Honda car is starting up near me or how about the unique sound of a Harley. If these characteristics point us to the manufacturer of these products, then could also the uniqueness of the separate interbreeding groups point us to a master designer that planned it that way?

Discussion Points

- ☐ Present all the evidence.
- ☐ Always separate fact from interpretation.
- ☐ Never falsify evidence.
- ☐ Do not discard alternate explanations for the evidence because of personal beliefs.

- Do you feel the above investigative rules are reasonable? If not, why do you feel that way?
- What do you think?
    - *Vestigial structures*: We have found uses for most of the structures. Will we find the purpose in those that remain as more time passes?
    - *Embryonic recapitulation*: Valid or Invalid?
    - *Similar structures*: Could these just indicate a similar purpose rather than a common ancestry?
    - *Atavistic structures*: Are these throwbacks to a previous existence or simply mistakes?
    - *Pepper moths*: You start with moths and end with moths. How does this prove evolution to different species?
    - *Adaptation:* Could a master designer to ensure the survival of the species in various environmental conditions just build this into a species?
    - *Fly mutations* – You start with flies and end with flies and the mutations are harmful to the flies. How does this evidence help the case for evolution?
    - *Hybrids* – Support for evolution or creation?

Chapter 5 – I Heard They Created Life in The Laboratory

In this chapter, I think I will add one more rule to our list of rules regarding evidence, *do not exaggerate*.

- ☐ Present all the evidence.
- ☐ Always separate fact from interpretation.
- ☐ Never falsify evidence.
- ☐ Do not discard alternate explanations for the evidence because of personal beliefs.
- ☐ **Do not exaggerate**.

This rule is perhaps broken more often than the others. Sometimes I think it may be done innocently in our zeal to explain things or fill in the gaps of evidence. Where it becomes much more damaging, however, is when we come to conclusions that require an incredibly exponential leap of faith. Suppose, for example, I made a single brick and then told you that I was about to produce a huge metropolitan city. Would you buy it? I do not think so.

Building Blocks

What does a brick have to do with creating life in the laboratory? Simply this, the creation of ridiculously small building blocks of life does not mean that we have proved the evolution of life any more than producing a single brick means that we are about to produce a huge metropolitan city. There have been many experiments over the years in which there have been exaggerated claims of being on the verge of proving or demonstrating the evolution of life.

Producing amino acids – In 1953, Dr. Stanley Miller managed to produce amino acids in a laboratory. It was quite a feat! However, producing some amino acids is a long way from producing a simple protein. The other parts of a living cell are far more complex than a simple protein and all the parts must be present simultaneously for life to exist. Isn't this an example of a brick to a metropolitan city exaggeration?

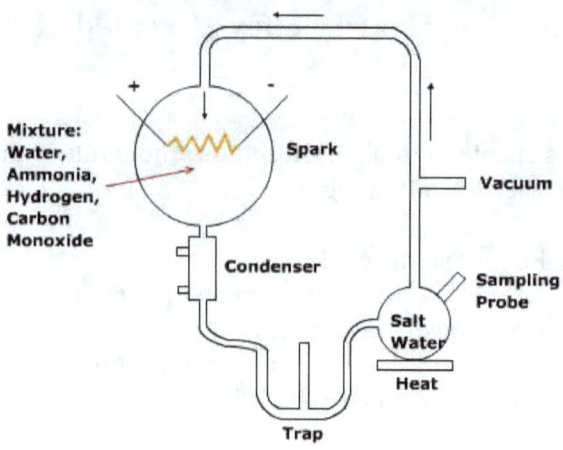

Dr. Miller's experiment was done with a different atmosphere than normally found on earth. The present atmosphere contains oxygen. He used ammonia, methane, hydrogen, and water vapor. His contention was that this kind of atmosphere might have existed on the primordial earth, but the oldest rocks seem to indicate there was a significant amount of oxygen present. Oxygen would destroy the newly created amino acids. He heated the mixture up to the boiling point and then allowed an electric charge to pass through the gases and produced a few amino acids. He constructed a cold trap to remove the products because the very charge that created them also destroyed the new molecules. They had to be quickly removed to preserve them. The mechanism would only produce a few kinds of amino acids, some of these were found in living things while others (right-handed amino acids) would interfere. Now we have a rare production mechanism to produce only a few usable amino acids that must have an even rarer trapping mechanism to pull them out of harm's way before they are destroyed. In calculating the probability of producing a simple protein by chance in chapter 2, I assumed that all possible amino acids were available. If they were not, the odds for producing life from simple elements just got exponentially larger.

Producing proteinoids – Dr. Sidney Fox managed to link a few amino acids together. He referred to these links as proteinoids. The linking process had to be done with dry amino acids at a temperature above the boiling point of water. Amino acids, however, cannot endure high temperatures for long. The addition of water would break apart the links reversing the reaction. These proteinoids had no real order to them and no usefulness. While a few links of amino acids might be produced in nature, they would break apart as soon as the sun came up and heated them up or if it started to rain. Ironically, water is necessary for life and yet it can be the cause of breaking down the building blocks of life. This, again, is a long way from creating life. The average protein contains hundreds of amino acid links all precisely ordered. A protein by itself is an incredibly long way from even the simplest cell. If I created a few soft bricks linked together in random order that could be easily destroyed with the first rain would I really be able to say I was on the verge of creating a large metropolitan city?

Designer Genes

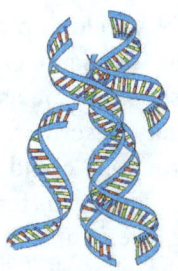

The DNA molecule containing the blueprint for reproducing life is an even greater problem. The DNA molecule is huge! Imagine it as an incredibly long spiraling ladder whose rungs are made up of four nucleotides arranged in a precise sequence. These nucleotides are like the letters of an alphabet. It is estimated that the human DNA contains about 3.5 billion nucleotides (3.5 billion letters). If the average book contained 350 words on a page with the average word about 10 letters long, it would have to be 10,000,000 pages long to be equivalent to the single DNA molecule. A section of this coding is referred to as a gene. There are 200,000 genes in the human body. A bunch of these genes together, sometimes in the thousands, control various organs in the body. If any of these genes contains an error, it could render the gene useless and create a problem (consider again the partial list of genetic disorders I referred to in chapter 3). With this level of complexity in the nucleus of the cell, it is no wonder that we have spent years trying to decipher the DNA code.

Studying the human genome is like trying to decipher a huge blueprint 10,000,000 pages long. It is well worth the effort, however, for it has led to some remarkable breakthroughs in understanding genes and what they control. This understanding is the first step in correcting some gene-related disorders by fixing the faulty genes. In fact, the DNA molecule has mechanisms to correct itself when an error is detected. However, scientists are far from knowing everything about the DNA code. They have correlated many of the gene sequences to specific protein production. There are large sections of the DNA molecule that they have not correlated to any protein production and have labeled such sections as "junk DNA". That is a mistake. Just because you do not know what the DNA section controls does not mean that it does not have a function. You simply may have not discovered it yet. For many years, the "junk DNA" was touted as leftover pieces from a previous evolutionary existence and presented as positive proof of evolution. Now, other scientists without the evolutionary bias are discovering many uses for these DNA segments. It appears that not only does DNA code to produce proteins, it also appears to code for the protein's usage. The same protein may be used in different ways with totally different results. Let me use an analogy here to make my point. A chemical engineer may describe on paper a process to produce glycerin. Another set of instructions could also be produced to turn that glycerin into harmless soap while a different set of instructions could document turning the same glycerin into highly explosive nitroglycerin. It all depends on the use of the glycerin. The DNA molecule is far more multidimensional and multifunctional than previously thought. Instead of calling something "junk", I believe it is much better to say that we just do not know the function.

    As I have been writing this book, the word processing software I am using detects and highlights errors in the writing. Sometimes it can be quite irritating. On my first attempt at the last sentence, I spelled the word irritating wrong and the software quickly pointed out my error. In some cases, the software makes the correction automatically. How many of you would regard such a software feature as just the product of chance changing the software? No, the programmers added it to aid the users. They placed a glossary in the program for comparison and programmed in the common language rules. When I write something that is not recognizable or breaks the rules, the software highlights the questionable part. If I ask, it then gives me some alternative spellings or suggestions. This is intelligence at work. In a similar way, the medical field hopes to use the natural repair processes within the DNA to repair defective genes, giving great hope for genetic cures. Can we really say, however, that exchanging good genes for bad ones is proof for evolution? Consider this, suppose you studied the Boeing 747 airplane and learned the function of every single part so that you could recognize and replace a faulty component. Would this prove that natural processes like wind, rain, lightning acting a pile of junk metal could make the 747? I do not think so. In fact, the study should tell us how incredibly impossible this would be. Every new complexity uncovered raises the improbability that such an action could happen by chance. Though we can replace an existing part, it just means we have achieved the ability to copy what already exists. Try starting from nothing and then show how the DNA molecule came into existence. That is what God had to do.

In the case of living things, even the copying process copies existing processes. Studying the DNA molecule mechanisms teaches us how corrections might be made. Is this evidence for mindless mechanisms producing life or the existence of a super designer creating life and backup mechanisms for maintaining it?

Controlling Cells

Synthesizing cells

Other studies have been done to create cells. To my knowledge, no one has succeeded in creating a cell from scratch. The closest anyone has ever come, has been to dismantle a cell and then put it back together again. Even to accomplish this feat, the experimenter had to use the very mechanisms within the cell to put it back together. These processes had to be in place before the experiment had any hope of success. How then can a cell ever be produced by chance acting on raw materials?

Stem cells

Before I leave the subject of cells, I need to say a word or two about stem cells. The stem cell is a basic cell. These cells are special cells that can be programmed to become a specific final cell type. The body can add to it or subtract from it what it needs to build any specific type of cell in the body. It can be programmed, for example, to become a red blood cell to carry oxygen in the body, a specific white blood cell to help fight disease, a skin cell, or any of a host of other cells. This potential has led many in the medical field to experiment with these cells to replace damaged cells. The medical possibilities are exciting. There have been some successes. They have been used to cure patients with leukemia and to repair damaged heart tissue. There is ongoing research in many other areas as well. The best results so far have not been with embryonic stem cells but rather adult stem cells.

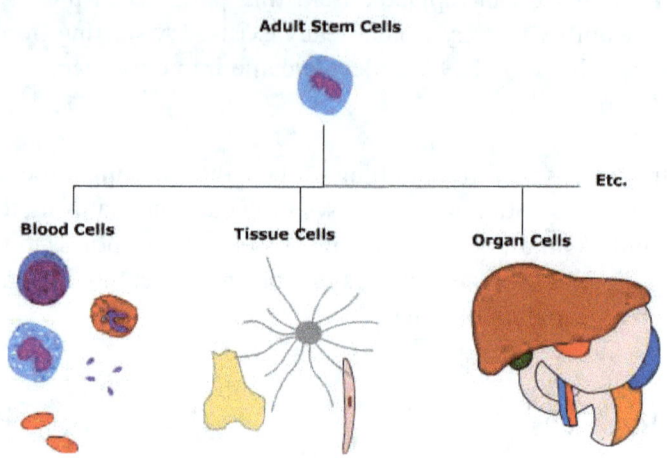

The following is an excerpt from a letter given to Congress on July 30, 2004 representing the feelings of over 2,000 medical professionals about the subject.

"To date, of course, embryonic stem cell research has yielded only very limited and/or questionable success in animal models and no therapeutic application whatsoever in human beings.

On the other hand, non-embryonic stem cells are ethically obtainable from multiple sources in human beings. Scientific research, funded by private and government sources, has shown significant progress in the last three years. Verified accomplishments of adult (non-embryonic) stem cell research is already providing hope and therapy for patients suffering from heart muscle injury, diabetes and brain damage from stroke- with realistic promise for treating other diseases on the horizon. Consider these research highlights:

- *'Adult' (non-embryonic) stem cells have been found in cord blood, placenta, bone marrow, fat, teeth and other sources.*

- *Adult stem cells found in one type of tissue can repair damage in another tissue type.*
- *Adult stem cells can be harvested from each patient, multiplied in culture and transplanted back into the patient.*
- *Adult stem cells work in multiple ways to repair damaged tissue.*
- *Since adult stem cells require limited, if any, manipulation, and are readily available from many sources, the cost for their clinical application will be far more reasonable than any application from embryonic stem cells.*
- *There are no ethical concerns in their use, making them acceptable to virtually all patients and healthcare providers and a bipartisan point of agreement for federal funding.*
- *Adult stem cells are already providing cures in animals and clinical human trials.*[13]

The fact that adult stem cells are available and hold great promise should not be surprising. We forget that we are dying and are continually in need of repair. The cells you have today in your body are not the cells you were born with. Those cells died a long time ago. They had to be replaced. Cells are continually dying. Red cells carrying oxygen only last about 120 days. Skin cells are continually flaking off. Infection, viruses, bacteria, and other things take their toll on our immune system. We are dying. The adult stem cells replace the worn-out parts and keep us going. We would not last more than a few weeks, at best, if they did not. Is the ability of stem cells to be programmed to replace worn out cells evidence for evolution or rather is it evidence for intelligent design?

My former employer, Beckman Coulter, (I am now retired) did not just produce instruments and reagents. The company also maintains a stock of spare parts. It is expected that over time certain parts of the system will wear out and need replacement. A large stock of parts is kept on hand for those parts receiving the most wear. Fewer parts are stocked for those that last longer. The company planned so that the instruments could easily be repaired when needed. This is intelligent planning. The company also

---

[13] "Support Adult Stem Cells". Christian Medical & Dental Associations, July 30, 2004. Letter to the U.S. Congress.

tries to make parts more uniform where possible so that fewer parts need to be stocked. This economizes space and saves money. The stem cell is the most elegant biological equivalent that I could ever think of. It is precisely what would be needed in the most compact form to produce replaceable parts for a failing biological system.

> Is this just chance or incredibly intelligent pre-planning?

Discussion Points

- Are scientists on the verge of discovering the biological mechanisms that could produce life by chance? Explain.

- The DNA molecule can correct itself. What do you think this feature indicates about its origin?

- Stem cells can be programmed to become a whole host of other cells needed in the body. Do you think this happened by chance or was planned? Explain.

CHAPTER 6 – All Those Fossils Prove Evolution is True, Don't They?

Imagine, for a moment, that you are rummaging through a huge junkyard full of all kinds of mechanical contraptions. What a goldmine! You are convinced this pile of junk allows you to fully examine the historical development of mechanized machines into their modern counterparts. You begin to categorize and organize your discoveries. You discover a unicycle wheel and then the remains of a two-wheeled pedal device. More digging yields a three-wheeled pedal device and later a large, elongated body also with three wheels. Maybe these wheel devices evolved one into another; from one to two to three and beyond. You become excited as you search further and discover many wheel devices. There is a two-wheeled machine with metal cylinders attached by a rod to a wheel that go up and down within another metal cylinder. Is this the next step upward in mechanical pedal evolution? The search of our junkyard continues to yield more interesting devices. Several four-wheeled devices with mechanical components, like the two-wheeled cylinders within a cylinder, are discovered. These machines come in different sizes. An eight-wheel device is found. A large three-wheeled machine is discovered with multiple-cylinder within cylinder devices with twisted blades attached to a central wheel. In another area, a multi-wheel device with wheels attached to wheels is uncovered. The excitement builds. After many more discoveries, you feel you have uncovered enough data to demonstrate the evolution of the mechanical device through time. You create and proudly display your carefully reasoned theory in a pictograph of your discoveries.

Because They Said So Isn't Good Enough

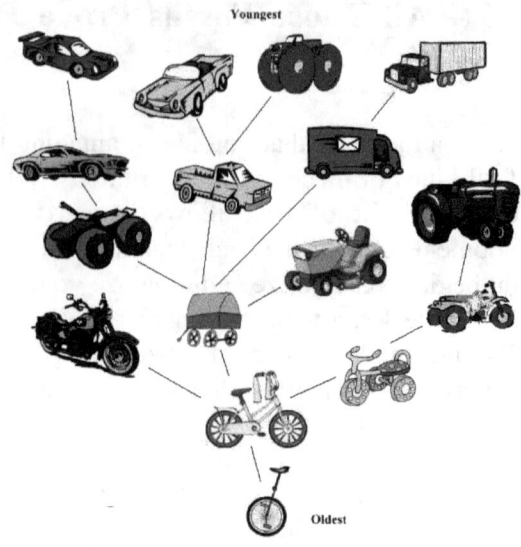

Later, the owner of the junkyard is interviewed, and he presents quite a different picture of how all the mechanical machines got there. You see the leaders in town decided it was time to clean up all the junk that had been lying around. The garages and sheds were emptied of all the things the kids had outgrown and the projects that folks never got around to completing. The front yards were cleaned up of all the junk cars. All the stuff was brought in in just a few days and piled up in the junkyard. You see, the mechanical devices in our hypothetical junkyard were really all in existence at the same time and brought together in short order. There was not a one to two to three to four-wheeled evolution of mechanized transportation. When we interview someone in the know, we find the theory to be false. While the theory, developed by extremely intelligent minds, was intriguing and highly imaginative, it was not true. Is it really any different with our junk pile of fossils?

We are going to look at the fossil evidence, but first let me remind you of the rules of evidence stated earlier. They are listed below:

- ☐ Present all the evidence.
- ☐ Always separate fact from interpretation.
- ☐ Never falsify evidence.
- ☐ Do not discard alternate explanations for the evidence because of personal beliefs.

We need to keep these in mind as we look at the fossil evidence. Before we do, though, let us take a moment or two to investigate just how a fossil is made.

Producing Fossils

The processes around us today really do not produce fossils. When an animal dies, it is eaten or crushed or worn away and eventually becomes dust. Consider a seashell in which the animal has died. The wind and waves roll it around on the bottom banging it into rocks and other debris on the bottom. Worms may come and drill holes into the shell further weakening the structure. Storms come and bang the shell hard against the rocks. It breaks apart. Over time, the once beautiful shell disintegrates into sand. If you think I am wrong here, just go to any seashore and examine what you see there. Despite this, however, fossil seashells are prolific in many areas of the world.

Other animals with even less outer protection than the seashell are eaten and destroyed more quickly. I once saw a cat that had died along the side of the road. It stayed there many days, so I thought that this might be a chance to see nature in action producing a future fossil. Alas, the only thing that happened in the days that followed was that the cat puffed up, then deflated, then decayed, and then gradually began to disappear. I thought I had another chance when an iguana got its tail caught in the trunk of a tree and died. Maybe nature would produce a fossil of the iguana. It never happened. The bones were stripped clean. Gradually, they began to break apart. The rain and wind began to wear the bones down and while there are still pieces left, I think they also will disappear over time.

The natural processes are destructive not preservative. This is especially true of the softer parts of plants and animals. Like the iguana, it is not long after an animal dies that all the soft tissue is gone. Yet, in fossils we find imprints of soft tissue. There are imprints of leaves, lilies, feathers and bats wings. Whole imprints of fish, soft corals, and insects are found. There are even preserved footprints of animals. How is this possible? Have you ever left your footprints in the sand? Not long after you create them the water and wind destroy them. Despite these destructive forces, fossils abound all over the world. I used to go hunting for them in rock quarries a few miles away from where I lived in Rochester, New York. I found huge beds of hard and soft corals in an area far away from the seashore. When I moved to Florida, it seemed that the whole state was one large fossil bed. I have read that fossils are found everywhere, even on the tops of mountains. Most of the fossil strata appear to involve water. Have you ever watched the seashore? The crashing waves do not preserve things. They smash and grind things up into sand not fossils, so how come there are so many fossils?

The answer is not that hard. Have you ever seen cement foundation, or sidewalk being poured? Did you put your hands in the cement and maybe write your initials in it? If the cement hardened, before it could be smoothed over, you just created a fossil imprint of your hand. That is exactly how soft tissue can be preserved as a fossil. It does not take a long time. In fact, the time must be short. If too much time passes, the cement will gradually fill in the depression and the imprint will disappear. It must happen quickly. There are beautiful intricate fossils all over the world, some of very fragile living things. Only sudden burial followed by hardening of the cementing materials would preserve such specimens. If this is true of these fossils, why could it not also be true of others as well? Maybe it does not take millions of years but only a short time. Remember the junkyard story at the beginning of this chapter.

Soft Bodied Living Things Found in Fossils

Predictions

While there are pointers to a quick burying of some living things to produce fossils, we cannot be certain of time frames. No one was there.

There are no videotapes or scientist notes to rely on. We do not have stop action photography. There are no eyewitnesses. The only thing we can do is to assume a theory is true and then make predictions about what should be seen. If there is more than one theory, do the same thing for each one. When we are finished, we simply observe the fossil record to see which theory seems to "get it right" most often. That theory is most likely the correct one. It still does not prove the theory true. It is still a matter of faith, but a faith that is much more easily defended than one that does not fit the evidence.

If evolution is true, what should we see in the fossil record? Since evolution is a gradual change from the simple organisms to more complex organisms, the fossil record should show the same gradual change from simple to more complex organisms. Evolution would take a considerable amount of time and the fossil beds would take a long time to produce. Therefore, it is reasonable to assume that the lowest layers would have the oldest fossils containing the simpler organisms. Layers on top should be younger and contain more complex organisms. To be sure, catastrophic processes in some areas can distort layers but there should be some evidence that a catastrophe occurred. The norm should be a clear delineation from the simple to the complex as we explore the lowest to the highest layers. The lowest layers should exhibit remarkably simple organisms arriving on the scene. As we move up the layers, there should be an increase in both the numbers and complexity of the fossils. Gaps may be present, but they should not be the rule.

On the other hand, if God, the master designer, created everything, He may not need a lot of time to complete the task. Our fossil "junkyard" may also not take a long time to produce and could be the result of catastrophic processes over a short period of time. In such a scenario, simple and complex organisms would all exist together at the same time. Therefore, a sudden burying of such organisms should produce a mixture of simple and complex throughout the layers. Differences from the lowest to the highest layers should reflect more the location of the organism at the time of burial, the ability of the organism to flee the catastrophic event, and anomalies in the catastrophe itself. Corals located at the bottom of the ocean, for example, are more likely to be at the bottom layers than say, birds that can fly away. Trees that can float in water are more likely to be found at higher layers than other living things that cannot float. If this God intended to keep groups of living things separated so they cannot interbreed, then there should be similar gaps between living things reflected in the fossil record. If this same God completed all creation prior to fossilization, then it is also likely that some of the fossilized remains may look quite like existing living things today. Those that do not have any living counterpart may simply reflect living things that are now extinct.

Now at this point, I have only given two example theories for the sake of simplicity. You may come up with others. These two reflect enough difference between them to come to some conclusion as to which is more defensible based on the actual fossil record. So now let's see what the fossils have to say.

The Fossil Evidence

The Precambrian rocks, which are the oldest rocks, are virtually devoid of fossils. There are a few reports of evidence of microscopic single cell organisms in these rocks but there are also those that dispute such claims. The Cambrian rocks above this layer explode with fossils representing almost all the various kinds of life except the vertebrates. Many of these are extraordinarily complex. Dr. Duane Gish describes this layer this way:

> *"In Cambrian rocks are found fossils of trilobites, sponges, brachiopods, worms, jellyfish, sea urchins, sea cucumbers, swimming crustaceans, sea lilies and other complex invertebrates. The appearance of this great variety of complex creatures is so startlingly sudden that it is commonly referred to as the "Cambrian explosion" in geological literature."*[14]

Used by permission. Copyright Illustra Media 2009[15]

---

14   Duane T. Gish, *Evolution: The Challenge of the Fossil Record* (El Cajon, CA: Creation Life Publishers Master Books Division, 1985), pp.54-55.
15   *Illustra Media.* "Darwin's Dilemma." 2009. DVD.

It is a jump from virtually nothing to incredible variety and complexity. Not exactly what you would expect from a gradual evolutionary change. In fact, the change is not gradual at all. There appear to be no intermediates. Life just seems to explode on the scene. It is also interesting that the species represented are largely those found at the bottom of the ocean with somewhat limited mobility. This is precisely what the Master Designer/Catastrophe model predicts would happen. The more mobile vertebrates such as fish, mammals, birds, etc. would exist at higher levels. They would be buried later.

Another interesting fact is that while some species no longer exist today (perhaps because of extinction), those that do exist look a lot like the modern counterparts. Sponges look like sponges, worms like worms, sea cucumbers like sea cucumbers, and so forth. If the evolutionary model is true, shouldn't we expect the modern counterparts to be more "evolved"? On the other hand, isn't this exactly what we would expect if a Master Designer had completed His creation?

Layers above the Cambrian do not provide very much (if any) evidence of intermediate forms either. There are great gaps between the invertebrates and fish, between fish and amphibians, between amphibians and reptiles, and between reptiles and mammals and birds. The gaps are so prevalent that even leading evolutionists have admitted they are real:

> *"The absence of fossil evidence for intermediary stages between major transitions in organic design, indeed our inability, even in our imagination, to construct functional intermediates in many cases, has been a persistent and nagging problem for gradualistic accounts of evolution."*[16]

> *"All paleontologists know that the fossil record contains precious little in the way of intermediate forms; transitions*

---

16 Stephen Jay Gould, "Is a New and General Theory of Evolution Emerging?" in *Paleobiology*, vol. 6(1) (1980), p. 127, referenced in *The Revised Quote Book*, ed. Dr. Andrew Snelling Ph.D. (Sunnybank, Brisbane, Australia: Creation Science Foundation Ltd., 1990), p. 8.

between major groups are characteristically abrupt."[17]

> "Despite the bright promise that paleontology provides a means of 'seeing' evolution, it has presented some nasty difficulties for evolutionists the most notorious of which is the presence of 'gaps' in the fossil record. Evolution requires intermediate forms between species and paleontology does not provide them. The gaps must therefore be a contingent feature of the record." [18]

> "In spite of these examples, it remains true, as every paleontologist knows, that most new species, genera, and families and that nearly all new categories above the level of families appear in the record suddenly and are not led up to be known, gradual, completely continuous transitional sequences."[19]

The gaps are, however, precisely what we would expect to see if the Master Designer/Catastrophe model is correct. Each species would have been a completed work just like an artist completes a painting or sculpture. The artist's brushstrokes and color patterns may look similar in different paintings yet, all the works would be distinct completed pieces. The artist does not remake an old painting or sculpture into a new one by making a few changes. He or she starts from scratch and makes the new work. In the same way, each new species in the fossil record appears suddenly. The gaps are huge. We do not have an evolutionary chain with a few missing links, we see a missing chain.

---

[17] Stephen Jay Gould, "The Return of Hopeful Monsters," in Natural History, vol. LXXXVI (6) (1980), p. 127, Ibid.

[18] David B. Kitts, Ph.D., "Paleontology and Evolutionary Theory," in *Evolution*, vol. 28 (1974), p. 467, Ibid, p. 9.

[19] George Gaylord Simpson, Ph.D., I *Major Features of Evolution* (New York: Columbia University Press, 1953), p. 360, Ibid, p. 9.

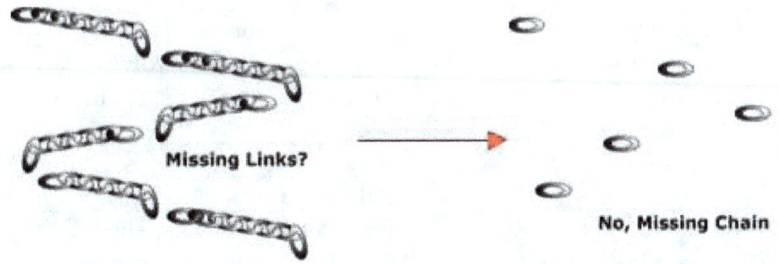

The carefully planned and executed works of a master designer model fit much better with the actual observed fossil record than the evolutionary model. Apparently, many evolutionists agree:

> *"In any case, no real evolutionist, whether gradualist or punctuationist, uses the fossil record as evidence in favor of the theory of evolution as opposed to special creation."*[20]

Such admissions should be insightful since the only real historical evidence for evolution would have to come from the fossil record!

Moving Up the Layers

As we move up the layers from the Cambrian, the same gap patterns persist. The same similarities to modern counterparts also persist as illustrated in the partial listing of the evolutionary geological timetable below:[21]

---

20 Mark Ridley, "Who doubts evolution?" in *New Scientist*, vol. 90 (1981), p. 831. Ibid.
21 Morris, *Scientific Creationism*, pp. 87-88.

Cenozoic 5-70 million years ago	Pliocene – horses, elephants
	Miocene – camels, wolves
	Oligocene – beavers, squirrels, ants
	Eocene – lemurs, rhinos
	Paleocene – rats, hedgehogs
Mesozoic 70-200 million years ago	Cretaceous – ducks, pelicans
	Jurassic – crocodiles, turtles
	Triassic – pines, palms
Paleozoic 200-600 million years ago	Permian – beetles, dragonflies
	Carboniferous - ferns, cockroaches
	Devonian – sharks, lungfish
	Silurian – scorpions, corals
	Ordovician – clams, starfish, worms
	Cambrian – sponges, snails, jellyfish

(Note: the ages are purely speculative based on the assumption of evolution.)

Clams, starfish, scorpions, corals, sharks, ferns all look like their living counterparts. The fossilized cockroach looks just as disgusting as the modern one. It is that way throughout the record. Dragonflies look like dragonflies. Crocodiles look like crocodiles. Pines look like pines. Turtles look like turtles and so forth.

Often, though, the older counterparts in the fossil record are bigger. Ancient sharks, for example, are often much larger than the modern ones. A tiger shark still has all the features of a tiger shark, just bigger. It appears that the ancient world was lusher with more abundant food supplies so that ancient species could grow larger. This data again supports the creation model and a downward trend in keeping with the second law of thermodynamics.

Some fossils may appear to not have the modern equivalent, but we must not be too hasty in judging these as transition or links between species. If a few of these species turn up one day that somehow did not completely die out, are they really transition forms? After all, if evolution is true, the more "evolved" species should be better able to compete and, eventually, push out the transition forms forcing them to die out. If they do exist today, are they transitional? The Coelacanth is sometimes considered a transitional form between the fish and the amphibian. If it was a transition form, shouldn't it have died out long ago? Instead, it has been caught on several occasions off the coast of Madagascar. A tsunami that devastated Southeast Asia washed up many weird deep ocean creatures along the beaches that could easily be classified as transitional or prehistoric forms. A few are shown in the following illustration.

If they still exist today, are they transitional or prehistoric? Could they not simply be designed by a master designer to exist in the deep dark waters of the ocean? Studies of these unique creatures often reveal some surprising survival abilities. For example, they often carry their own light source to better see in the dark. Others can gather food by mimicking certain luminescent phytoplankton to lure unsuspecting fish into a trap. Others can survive in very warm waters or very cold. Are these traits really the result of gradual evolution or were they designed that way by a master designer? You see, there is more than one explanation here. They may appear weird to us, but they may be perfectly constructed to live and survive in their own environment.

Which leads to another question, how do we know how old the rocks are that contain these so-called transitional forms?

Dating the Rocks

The next chapter will expand on some dating methods, but one, using index fossils, really fits more with the study of the fossils. The idea is to assume evolution is true and then "estimate" a time scheme for the process to occur from the ancient one-celled organisms through invertebrates, to vertebrates, to fish, to amphibians, and so forth. Now if you find a fossil of an extinct living thing that appears to fit into your framework as a transition form, you date the rock accordingly. Now of course, all the dating schemes are pure conjecture, the figment of some highly active imaginations. Remember, no one was there. There is no eyewitness evidence.

Many rocks on display that contain such fossils often have display cards claiming the rock is so many "millions of years old". None of these dates can be proven. How then can we state such dates as true? If the underlying assumption is not true, then the whole dating method is not true.

This dating method is often used as proof of evolution. The idea is illustrated below:

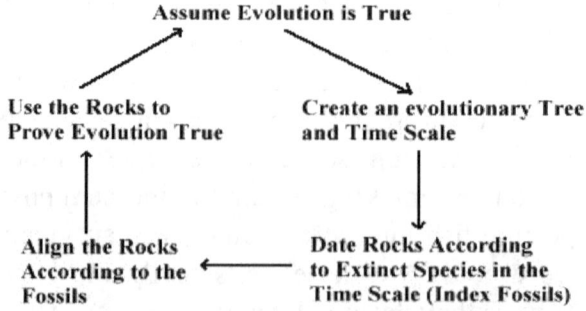

This kind of reasoning is circular. Now we might justify it to an extent if the fossil layers lined up from bottom to top in the same order as our assumed time framework. But do they?

The Layer Order

First, nowhere in the world do we find all the periods described in the textbooks all in one place

Second, there are many areas of the world that older rocks as dated by the fossils appear on top of younger ones. Dr. John C. Whitcomb and Dr. Henry M. Morris have documented many areas of the world in which formations are out of sequence.

> *"In every mountainous region on every continent, there seem to be numerous examples of supposedly 'old' strata superimposed on top of 'young' strata. In the absence of definite structural evidence to the contrary, one would naturally suppose that the lowermost strata must necessarily have been first deposited and, therefore, be 'older.' But the fossils often seem to belie this assumption, and it is the fossils which govern the assigned formation age."*[22]

Many of these areas are huge, the size of mountains and even small states.

> *"To illustrate the character of these important areas, we might consider the well-known Heart Mountain Thrust of Wyoming. This supposed thrust occupies roughly a triangular area, 30 miles wide by 60 miles long, with its apex at the northeast corner of Yellowstone Park. It consists of about 50 separate blocks of Paleozoic strata (Ordovician, Devonian, and Mississippian) resting essentially horizontally and conformably on Eocene beds, some 250,000,000 years younger!"*[23]

---

22   Dr. John C. Whitcomb and Dr. Henry M. Morris, *The Genesis Flood* (The Presbyterian and Reformed Publishing Company, 34th printing, 1990), p. 180.
23   Ibid, p. 181.

The layers conform or are in harmony with each other. There is no evidence that the "older" rocks were pushed up and over the "younger ones" and there should be. This is not an isolated example. Whitcomb and Morris document other huge areas of supposedly older rocks on top of younger ones including:

> *The Lewis overthrust of Montana (about 350 miles wide and 6 miles thick displaced at least 35 or 40 miles).*[24]
> *The Matterhorn in Switzerland (moved supposedly some 30 to 60 miles).*[25]

Such over thrusting if it did occur, would be an incredibly powerful catastrophic event.

> *"It is recognized that phenomena of this sort have taken place on a small scale, in certain localities where there is ample evidence of intense faulting and folding. However, these visible confirmations of the concept are on a small scale, usually in terms of a few hundreds of feet, whereas many of the great overthrust areas occupy hundreds or even thousands of square miles. It seems almost fantastic to conceive of such huge areas and masses of rocks really behaving in such a fashion, unless we are ready to accept catastrophism of an intensity that makes the Noachian Deluge seem quiescent by comparison!"*[26]

> Did you get that? On the one hand scientists reject Noah's flood as a real event but then turn around and accept that a greater catastrophic event may have occurred to push huge areas of the world up and over others. Is this really science?

24	Ibid, pp. 186-187.
25	Ibid, p. 199.
26	Ibid, p. 180.

Remember our junkyard illustration at the beginning of this chapter? The fossil situation is much like finding our unicycle on the top of the heap and the cars and trucks at the bottom, older on top of younger. Such ordering, however, would be expected and even predicted if all the living things were contemporary and a giant cataclysm (like a world-wide flood) created a huge slurry of living things that then settled out into the fossil layers.

Anomalies

Occasionally anomalies are found in the strata that are simply not easily, if at all, explained by gradual forming of layers over eons of time. Some of these finds are ignored. Others are written off as frauds without ever really investigating their authenticity. In either case, is this really science? Should we not be investigating all evidence and draw our conclusions accordingly? If the evidence does not support preconceived ideas, then maybe it is time to change our ideas. Let me use one example to illustrate worldview bias. In the Paluxy Riverbed near Glen Rose Texas, two sets of prints were found. One set appears to be dinosaur, the other set appeared to be human footprints near those of the dinosaur. The dinosaur prints are generally accepted as real and dated about 140 million years old. There is disagreement as to whether the other tracks were made by man. Whether they were real or not isn't the point. It is the reaction I heard from a scientist evaluating the find that disturbs me. He basically said that if he found the second set of prints by themselves, he would conclude that they were human footprints. He then went on to say that because they were found next to the dinosaur footprints, they could not possibly be human. Evolutionists have long criticized the creationists for their bias while at the same time failing to realize that they are just as biased.

If such footprints are real, the whole evolutionary scenario is really in question. How could man, supposedly beginning only a few million years ago, exist with dinosaurs that existed 140 million years ago? The timeframes must be way off. Perhaps the dinosaurs existed much closer to modern times. If they did, it would explain the worldwide stories of dragons and the modern sightings of huge creatures like the Loch Ness monster. It would also explain the biblical references to huge creatures that roamed the earth and sea.

> *"Look now at the behemoth, which I made along with you; He eats grass like an ox. See now, his strength is in his hips, and his power is in his stomach muscles. He moves his tail like a cedar; the sinews of his thighs are tightly knit. His bones are like beams of bronze, His ribs like bars of iron."* (Job 40:15-18)

> *"Can you draw out Leviathan with a hook, or snare his tongue with a line which you lower? Can you put a reed through his nose or pierce his jaw with a hook?" ... "Can you fill his skin with harpoons, or his head with fishing spears? Lay your hand on him; remember the battle – never do it again! Indeed, any hope of overcoming him is false; Shall one not be overwhelmed at the sight of him? No one is so fierce that he would dare stir him up..."* (Job 41:1,2, 7-10a)

Perhaps "behemoth" and "leviathan" still exist somewhere today. I wonder...

Such fossil finds are easily explained if they all were created together and then a catastrophe buried the evidence.

Trees found vertically crossing several layers – There are many places where trees are found vertically through several layers of strata. Some of these trees are found at different heights within the strata. The standard evolutionary explanation is that forests existed at different time periods separated by periods of destruction and deposition. Such fossils, however, would not exist if it took a long time to produce the layers. The trees would have simply decayed or weathered away long before all the layers were in place.

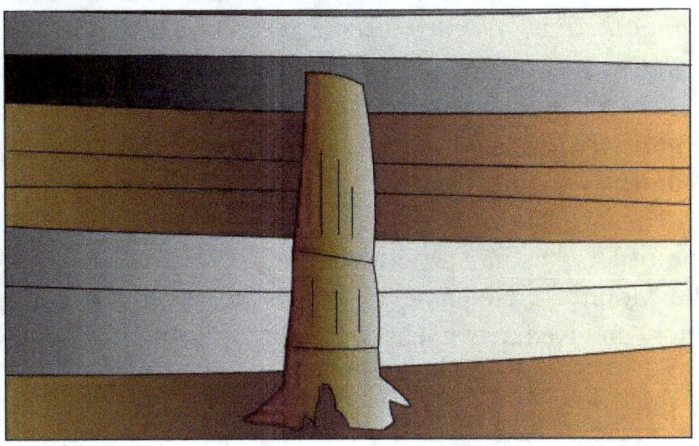

Can such events occur quickly though? On May 18, 1980, Mount St. Helens exploded and produced an incredible geologic event that should change geologist's thinking on this very topic. The mountain exploded, flattened a forest, and created a tidal wave in nearby Spirit Lake. The energy output was about the equivalent of 20,000 Hiroshima-size atomic bombs. The waves washed incredible amounts of mud and logs into the lake. The result was mud strata up to 600 feet thick created in a matter of days not millions of years. According to Steven A. Austin, Ph.D. who has been to the area, the floating trees occupy about 2 square miles of the lake surface.[27] Many of the trees have gradually become waterlogged and sunk to the bottom. To quote from Dr. Austin's article:

27   Steven A. Austin, Ph.D., "Mount St. Helens and Catastrophism" in *Impact*, Article no. 157 (1986), p. iii.

> *"Hundreds of upright floated and deposited logs have been grounded in shallow water along the shore of the lake. These trees, if buried in sediment, would appear to have been a forest which grew in place over hundreds of years, which is the standard geological interpretation for the upright petrified 'forests' at Yellowstone National Park...*
>
> *Scuba investigation of the upright deposited trunks shows that some are already solidly buried by sedimentation, with more than three feet of sediment around their bases, while others have no sediment around their bases. This proved that the upright trees were deposited at different times, with their roots buried at different levels. If found buried in the stratigraphic record, these trees might be interpreted as multiple forests which grew on different levels over periods of thousands of years."*[28]

The date of Dr. Austin's article was July 1986, a little over 6 years after the Mount St. Helens event. Can such events occur quickly? Absolutely and we have at least one modern geologic event to prove it.

Evidence of man found in coal – A human skull was found in coal in the early 1800's.[29]

On June 11, 1891, the Morrisonville, Illinois Times reported the finding of an intricately formed gold chain inside a chunk of coal.[30] Now and then, such stories do appear, and they are extremely hard to prove as true. We do not have video or documentary evidence to show the coal being broken open and the find exposed. We only have the word of the discoverer. Coal beds are often dated as 70 plus million years old. If the story is true, how did a gold chain obviously made by man (no animal can produce it) get imbedded in a chunk of coal? Again, the answer is easy. If man existed at the beginning and

---

28   Ibid.
29   Whitcomb and Morris, Ibid, pp. 175-176.
30   George Mulfinger, "The Flood and the Fossils", *Bob Jones University Press*, p. 5.

a catastrophe buried him and his belongings along with the animals and plants existing at that time.

The standard evolutionary textbooks indicate that coal formation was formed from peat in swamps and therefore is a slow process. The events cited in the previous section on Spirit Lake near Mount St. Helens may indicate differently. Again citing Dr. Austin:

> *"The enormous log mat floating on Spirit Lake has lost its bark and branches by the abrasive action of wind and waves. Scuba investigations of the bottom showed that water-saturated sheets of tree bark are especially abundant on the bottom of the lake, where, in areas removed from volcanic sediment added from the lake shore, a layer of peat several inches thick has accumulated. The Spirit Lake peat resembles, both compositionally and texturally, certain coal beds of the eastern United States, which also are dominated by tree bark and appear to have accumulated beneath floating log mats."*[31]

These huge mats of floating logs would be exactly what you would expect to find because of a huge catastrophic flood. The receding waters would contain the logs in certain areas where coal deposits could form rapidly. If man existed at the same time, then it should be quite possible to find evidence of man's existence in the coal beds.

Soft Tissue in Dinosaur Bones – There have been recent discoveries of soft tissue such as DNA, bone marrow, and blood cells inside dinosaur bones. Such discoveries are extremely problematic for the evolutionist. Dinosaurs supposedly died out about 65 million years ago. Soft tissue, however, can only survive on the order of thousands of years. How then could such tissue still exist within the bones? Scientists also found that this was not a rare event. When they began cutting open additional dinosaur bones, they often found the same thing. Evolutionists offered explanations but ignored the simplest explanation of all, the bones are not that old.

---

31   Austin, Ibid, p. iii.

Because They Said So Isn't Good Enough

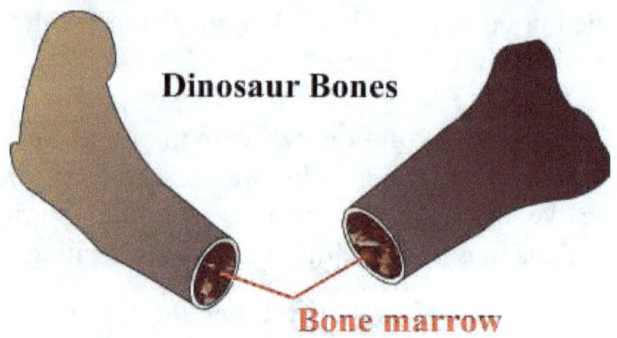

Missing Links – Periodically, we will hear in the news media of some new discovery of another missing link in the so-called evolution of man. There will be a lot of hype for a while and some scientist will undoubtedly become famous and even have the discovery, perhaps, named after him or her. When we hear such things, though, we need to be a bit more discerning. Questions should be asked. What was discovered and where? If the item is dated, what was the basis for the determining the date? Why is it considered a missing link or is this just another interpretation of a find based on the assumption that evolution is true? After the scientists have had a chance to reflect on the discovery for a while, what do they now say? The latter question does not always make it into the media.

If we placed all the finds to date, we may have trouble covering up a good-sized dining room table. Whole skeletons are rarely found. The finds are generally small fragments: skull, a limb, some teeth, etc. Yet incredible conclusions are drawn from very skimpy evidence. Let us look at a few examples to illustrate.

- ***Ramapithecus*** – This fossil evidence was discovered in 1932 in northwestern India by G.E. Lewis. Later, others discovered fossil remains in other areas of the world. The fossil evidence that led the scientists to classify the remains as hominid (human ancestor) was largely based on a few teeth and some jaw fragments. After much wrangling about whether these remains should be classified as ape-like or more human-like, they were placed in the ape family. Dr.

Gish had this to say about these fossils:

"As we will see later, Ramapithecus is just one of a long series of creatures that have been suggested at one time or another as 'missing links' but which, when more complete evidence became available, were relegated to the ape family."[32]

- ***Australopithecus*** – There were many finds that were classified in this group with names like *africanus* and *robustus*. Louis Leakey and his wife discovered one find and gave it the name *Zinjanthropus bosei* (East-Africa Man). They appeared to be much more ape-like than anything else.

"All of these animals possessed small brains, the cranial capacity averaging 500 c.c. or less, which is in the range of a gorilla, and about one-third of that for man. These animals thus unquestionably had the brains of apes, regardless of what else can be said about them. Both of them had ape-like skulls and jaws, these features being particularly obvious in the case of A. robustus."[33]

In 1973, near Hadar in Ethiopia, anthropologists lead by Donald Johanson discovered another find like A. africanus. It was female, and he declared it to be hominid and gave it the name "Lucy". He became famous overnight. The newspapers at that time expressed the sensational claims of Johanson and his group. There were many other finds in the area later all sensational. You would have thought that they had discovered true missing links and absolutely proved evolution true. But did they? Lucy's brain size was only 380cc to 450 cc and she was about three and a half feet tall. After the initial sensationalism of the finds, however, there was a lot of debate and criticism that did not make it into the newspapers. Dr. Gish summarizes the findings:

---

[32] Gish, *Evolution: The Challenge of the Fossil Record*, p. 144.
[33] Gish, Ibid, p. 145.

"We conclude that the autralopithecines (A. africanus, H. africanus. H. habilis, A. bosei, A. robustus, A. afarensis) were apes, with no genetic relationship either to Man or to any extinct apes. Their mode of locomotion, while unique in some respects, was probably more like that of the orangutans than that of any other living creature."[34]

- **Homo Erectus** –The first discovery of fossils now classified as Homo Erectus was in the late 1800's by a Dutch physician, Eugene Dubois. He first found a skull cap in Java. Then about a year later he found a femur near the original find and then three teeth. He was convinced he had found a missing link and named it Pithecanthropus erectus, which means erect ape-man. The find became known as "Java Man". The cranial capacity according to Dubois was about 900 cc. At the time he also discovered two modern human skulls in the same area that he failed to report. Some felt that Java Man was man-like, but others felt he resembled a giant ape. Later, Dubois himself agreed with the latter conclusion. How then can Java Man be considered a missing link?

Another discovery fitting into the Homo Erectus classification was found about 25 miles from Peking, China. Several skull fragments, mandibles, and teeth were found in the 1920s and 1930s. The creature was called Sinanthropus pekinensis ("Peking Man"). There were stories that modern man remains were also found in the same area. Most of the evidence was lost during World War II so there is no way to examine the evidence today. Dr. Gish had this to say about this situation:

"As a result, we are totally dependent on models and descriptions of this material left by a few investigators, all of whom were totally committed to the idea that man had evolved from animal ancestors. Even if a scientist is completely honest and as objective as humanly possible, the model or description he fashions based on scanty and incomplete material will reflect to a critical degree what he

---

[34] Gish, Ibid, p. 179.

thinks the evidence ought to show."[35]

Preconceived notions about truth do not make something true. All the evidence should be considered and all the explanations before arriving at a conclusion. I won't belabor the point but two famous "intermediates are worth noting:

- **Neanderthal man** –This find was first discovered over 100 years ago in a cave near Dusseldorf, Germany. He was considered brutish and sub-human. On further examination of the bones, it was discovered he suffered from rickets causing softening of the bones and was malformed as a result. His cranial capacity was greater than that of modern man. Was he sub-human or really a modern man with a vitamin deficiency? Look around you. Imagine the skulls of some of the people you see. If you discovered their skull some time in the future, how would you classify them? I cannot help but chuckle at some of the people I have observed. I have seen two models of what Neanderthal Man must have looked like. In one, he appeared retarded and in the other he looked like a college professor. Today he is classified as fully human.

- **Cro-Magnon Man** –This man classified as Homo sapiens (modern man) and may have had a cranial capacity larger than modern man. He appeared to be much like the modern Europeans but appeared in the textbooks as though he was intermediate between ancient apes and modern man.

Before we buy into the next big discovery as a missing link in the evolution of man, I would suggest we all try a simple experiment. Look at the people around you: the man at the gas station, the woman at the grocery store, your college professor. Imagine you found their skeletons many years from now after they have died. Would any of their skulls be unusual? Would some of their limbs appear intermediary between an ape and modern man? How about their teeth? You could do the same

---
35   Gish, Ibid, p. 187.

mental experiment with some of the apes and monkeys at the zoo. I think I could find virtually all the so-called missing links living among us today in some form or another!

Bloopers

There have been mistakes made, some of which stayed in the textbooks for years.

- *Nebraska Man* —William Jennings Bryan used this find in the famous Scopes trial to defend the teaching of evolution in the schools. It was supposed to be a missing link between a chimpanzee and modern man. It was only based on the finding of a single tooth that was later identified as originating from an extinct pig. It was amazing how a single tooth could be transformed into a brutish-looking illustration which was published in the Illustrated London News.[36]

- *Piltdown Man* – Experts dated this find at about 500,000 years old and consisted of a very ape-like jaw with a human-like skull. Later, a method was developed to date fossil bones based on the amount of fluoride absorbed by the bones from the soil. When the two parts were analyzed, the skull was dated at a few thousand years old while the jaw was dated at about a year old. Further investigation revealed that the bones had been treated with iron salts to make them look old and that the teeth had been filed. It was a hoax! Nevertheless, it was in the textbooks for over thirty years as positive proof that evolution was true.

People will go to great lengths to prove their preconceived ideas true. Scientists are no different. The two preceding examples occurred in the first half of the twentieth century. Dr. Gish made this comment on this tendency:

"Have things changed much today? Two recent examples tend to indicate that tendencies of authorities haven't really

---
[36] Gish, Ibid, p. 187.

changed much at all. An article in Science News relates the charges of Tim White that Noal Boaz has mistaken a dolphin's rib for the clavicle (shoulder bone) of a hominoid. White jests that the fossil should be designated Flipperpithecus!

A UPI press release published May 14, 1984, revealed that a skull fragment which had been hailed by experts one year earlier as the oldest human fossil ever found in Europe may have come from a donkey!"[37]

I will refrain from commenting on the last example, although it is tempting.

---

37   Gish, Ibid, p. 190.

Discussion Points

- Fossil production is not the norm today. What different events in the past could produce the prolific number of fossils we see?

- How do you explain the incredible complexity and variety in the Cambrian layers?

- What do you think is the best explanation for the sudden appearance of new species without fossilized intermediates?

- What do you think is the best explanation for old fossil species looking a lot like their modern counterparts?

- Can we date rocks using index fossils and then use the rocks to prove evolution is true? Explain.

- What do you think is the best explanation of apparent older rocks (evolutionary viewpoint) on top of younger rocks?

- What do some of the discussed anomalies indicate about the evolutionary time scale?

- Which model, evolution or creation, seems to fit better the observed fossil record? Explain.

CHAPTER 7 – Dating and Time

As indicated in the previous chapter, the dating of rocks is often based on the assumption that evolution is true. The paths from simple organisms to modern man are postulated timeframes that are assigned. Those fossil bearing rocks are then dated based on how the fossils they contain fit into those timeframes. This kind of dating is highly subjective. It cannot be stated as true unless there is independent, more objective confirmation of the time. This confirmation is vital. While the creation model does not require long timeframes, the evolution model does. Since we cannot see evolution taking place (i.e. the changing of one organism into another) if it occurs, the change must occur slowly over a long period of time.

Radiometric Dating

Scientists have sought confirmation of the long timeframes in a general technique referred to as radiometric dating. The idea, as diagrammed below, is that a radioactive parent element decays into a more stable even non-radioactive daughter element. If the rate of decay can be estimated, then an attempt can be made to estimate the age of a rock containing the parent and daughter elements.

Parent Element
Ex. Uranium ^{238}

Decay Rate

Daughter Element
Ex. Lead^{206}

Note: the previous diagram greatly oversimplifies the steps for the sake of clarity. In fact, the Uranium^{238} decay is believed to go through about 14 steps to reach the final product of Lead^{206}.

This technique is based on three assumptions:

1. The amount of parent and daughter material in the rock at the time it was formed is known.
2. The rate of decay is constant and predictable.
3. The rock is a closed system and no parent or daughter material can enter or leave the rock.

The dating method rests on these assumptions like standing on a three-legged stool. If any of these assumptions fail, the "stool" falls, and the conclusions cannot be relied upon as true. To better understand why, let's use an analogy. Suppose you walk into a kitchen and find a basin of water in the sink with an overturned box of salt on the countertop. You notice salt crystals every so often falling into the water. We might think that we can determine how long the basin has been in the sink by determining the rate at which the salt crystals are falling into the basin and measuring the amount of salt in the water.

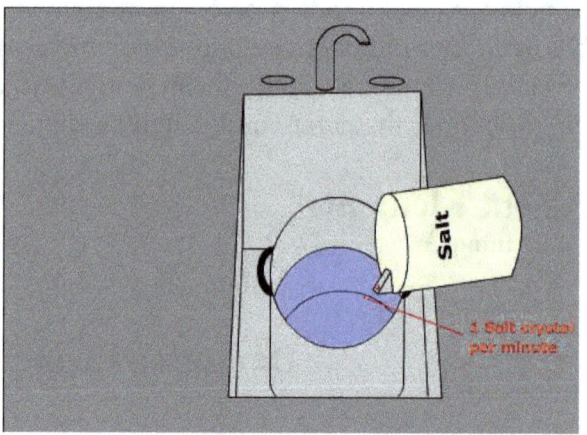

Now let us suppose we did this, and we determined, for the sake of simplicity, that the crystals are falling into the water at the rate of one crystal a minute. Now suppose we measured the amount of salt content and found it to be equivalent to 1,000 grains of salt. Our basin then must have been in the sink for 1,000 minutes. Now let us suppose that before we entered the room, the earth shook a little bit vibrating the countertop and caused the box of salt to tip over.

When it did, 350 grains of salt fell into the basin. You see, the rate of salt falling into the water was not constant. It accelerated at the beginning and then decreased. Now our apparent age really is only about 650 minutes because 350 grains fell in one minute instead of the measured 1 grain when we entered the room. Now suppose that we observed a bit before the box fell over that someone placed the basin in the sink, poured 500 grains of salt into it and set the box of salt on the counter. Now the entire age of the basin is reduced to just 150 minutes. What if, unbeknown to us, 145 grains fell into the basin from a different source while the basin was in the sink? Now the time is reduced to just 5 minutes. Since we started observing and measuring when we entered the room, we can have no knowledge of any of the events. Our conclusion based on our assumptions is 1,000 minutes while the actual time is only 5 minutes. Our assumptions were wrong. We did not see how much salt was added to the basin right at the beginning, the rate change as the box of salt fell over, and the additional source of the salt. These same kinds of errors can also be inherent in radiometric dating.

Let us take each assumption in turn and see why.

Assumption 1 – The amount of parent and daughter material in the rock at the beginning is known.

Most radiometric dating methods assume no daughter material in the rock at the beginning. There is absolutely no way to determine the amount of daughter material that existed at the beginning unless we could enter a time machine and go back in time and measure the rock when it was formed. If there was daughter material present when the rock was formed, the rock will appear to be incredibly old just seconds later. Our basin appeared to be in the sink for 500 minutes just seconds after it was placed there, and salt added.

Assumption 2 – The rate of decay is constant and predictable.

The rate of decay is expressed in terms of half-life; the time it takes for half of the parent material to decay into the daughter material. The assumption is that this half-life remains constant so that it can be used to estimate the age of a rock. Decay rates have been shown to be changeable depending on the environment surrounding the rock. Anything that can penetrate and influence the atomic structure can influence the decay rate. If there were an increase in cosmic radiation, for example, wouldn't this also stress the atoms and increase the decay rate? Proximity to the same or other sources of radiation could also affect the decay rate. If you spread a few pounds of Uranium out on a lawn the only thing that may happen is that you get bombarded with some radiation (over time it could be lethal). Take the same uranium and pack it tightly together and it blows up the city you live in. You have created an atomic bomb. The decay rate did not remain constant. The closeness to other sources of radiation will influence the decay rate.

If the half-life is exceedingly long (for Uranium^{238} it is about 4.5 billion years), how can we be sure that the radiation environment remained constant throughout all time? Remember the salt analogy; the rate of salt entering the basin changed when the box fell over. For that matter, how can we be sure the half-life is even correct? We are only measuring for an extremely short time interval to deduce the rate. Some scientists are beginning to acknowledge that these rates may not be as predictable as we think:

> *"The age of our globe is presently thought to be some 4.5 billion years, based on radio decay rates of uranium and thorium. Such 'confirmation' may be short-lived, as nature is not to be discovered quite so easily. There has been in recent years the horrible realization that radio decay rates are not as constant as previously thought, nor are they immune to environmental influences.*
>
> *And this could mean that the atomic clocks are reset during some global disaster, and events which brought the Mesozoic to a close may not be 65 million years ago but, rather, within*

the age and memory of man."[38]

> "At any temperature or pressure, collisions with stray cosmic rays or the emanations of other atoms may cause changes other than those of normal disintegration. It seems very possible that what is called 'spontaneous disintegration' of radioactive elements is related in some way to the action of cosmic rays and, if so, the rate of disintegration may vary from century to century according to the intensity of the rays. The evidence for a strongly increasing change in the cosmic ray influx is most favorable in the light of Dr. T. G. Barnes' investigation of the decay of the earth's magnetic field."[39]

Assumption 3 - The rock is a closed system and no parent or daughter material can enter or leave the rock.

Rocks are not closed systems. They are subject to environmental influences. Every time it rains, water can seep into a rock and affect the rock contents. Gasses produced because of radioactive decay can escape from a rock. If a rock is more porous, other materials can be deposited into it or leached from it. They are just not isolated from the effects of the environment. The uranium-lead dating method is not immune. According to Dr. Henry M. Morris:

> "Uranium is easily leachable by groundwater, for example. The intermediate element, radon gas, can easily move in or out of a uranium system. There are, in fact, various ways by which the components of this type of system can enter or leave it."[40]

Another interesting fact is that the daughter material can come from other sources other than the radioactive decay. In the uranium to lead model, for example, some lead can be changed into

---

[38] Frederic B. Jueneman, FAIC, "Secular catastrophism," as quoted by *The Quote Book #96* (Industrial Research and Development, 1982), p. 21.
[39] Harold S. Slusher, M.S., "Critique of Radiometric Dating," in *ICR Technical Monograph No. 2* (San Diego, CA: Creation-Life Publishers, Inc, 1973), p.18.
[40] Morris, *Scientific Creationism*, p.140.

other forms through neutron capture and may not necessarily come from radioactive decay.

> *"An even more important phenomenon by which these balances can be upset is that of 'free neutron capture,' by which free neutrons in the mineral's environment may be captured by the lead in the system to change the isotopic value of the lead. That is, lead 206 may be converted into Lead 207, and Lead 207 into Lead 208 by this process. It is perhaps significant that Lead 208 usually constitutes over half the lead present in any given lead deposit. Thus, the relative amounts of these 'radiogenic' isotopes of lead in the system may not be a function of their decay from thorium and uranium at all, but rather a function of the amount of free neutrons in the environment."*[41]

This situation is exactly like our salt into the basin of water analogy where salt is entering the basin from other sources.

Other radioactive decay methods do not fare any better. The Potassium-Argon method most widely used for dating rocks is even more open to the environment. Potassium can combine with other elements to form salts that can be easily dissolved out of rocks. The Argon gas can move into and out of rocks at will. The Rubidium-Strontium dating method suffers from the same difficulties. Rubidium can be leached out of a rock and strontium can be added to the rock from other sources. Rocks are simply not closed systems.

> *"The potassium-argon ages of meteorites investigated ranged from 5×10^9 years to 15.6×10^9 years... As much as 80 percent of the potassium in a small sample of iron meteorite can be removed by distilled water in 4.5 hours"*[42]

So, if a meteorite is not old enough to serve our purposes, we could just soak it in distilled water to age it a bit more. We could go

---
41 Ibid, pp. 141-142.
42 Ibid. p. 146 [quoting L.A. Rancitelli and D.E. Fisher "Potassium-Argon Ages of Iron Meteorites," *Planetary Science Abstracts* (48th Annual Meeting of the American Geophysical Union, 1967), p. 167].

on and on about the various methods and see the same thing in all of them. If this is true, then how can we rely on any ages derived from such methods?

The fact of the matter is that we cannot. Consider an example of dating some relatively modern volcanic rocks:

> "*Sidney P. Clementson, a British engineer, has recently made a detailed study of such modern volcanic rocks and their uranium 'ages,' as published in Soviet geophysical journals and other papers, and has shown that in all such cases the uranium-lead ages were vastly older than the true ages of the rocks. Most of them gave ages of over a billion years, even though the lava rocks were known to have been formed in modern times.*"[43]

I searched the Internet one day to see what anyone had to say on the subject and found one article claiming that it was not fair to the dating method to use such a young rock. They claimed that the natural lead fooled the dating method and that the method was not made for such young ages. I believe they missed the point, though. How can we ever know what portion of the daughter material was just there from the beginning? Any rock that has natural lead in it (lead not from radioactive decay), will appear incredibly old the day it was made. Perhaps all the rocks are like that and our "old" rocks simply are not old at all. Now we might consider the methods a bit more creditable if different methods agreed with each other when applied to the same samples. That too appears not to be the case.

> "*It is common to find that the several ages that are obtainable from a suite of uranium-thorium-lead isotopes are either discordant among themselves or 'anomalous' with respect to the assumed age of the formation. Therefore, they must be either corrected to the assumed 'true' age or discarded as hopelessly discrepant.*"[44]

---

43 Morris, *Scientific Creationism*, p. 143.
44 Morris, *Scientific Creationism*, p. 144.

The last statement in the previous quote is really revealing. You cannot assume an age for a rock and then try to make the measurements agree with that assumption. You also cannot use the assumption as the basis for accepting or rejecting the measurement. That is not science. Remember the Scientific Method? Are we not supposed to modify our assumptions and theories based on our observations and not the other way around?

> Shouldn't we also recognize the limits of our ability to prove our theories and not insist that others embrace them in the absence of such proofs?

Radiocarbon Dating

Radiocarbon dating is another method of dating that is well respected in the scientific community. It was invented by Dr. Willard Libby and earned him a Nobel Prize. The method is based on measuring the ratio of the unstable Carbon-14 to Carbon-12 in a material. Carbon-14 is produced in the upper atmosphere as the result of bombarding Nitrogen-14 atoms with cosmic radiation. The Carbon-14 then decays with a half-life of about 5,730 years. It is believed that the ratio of Carbon-14 to Carbon-12 in the atmosphere is constant and reacts chemically just like Carbon-12. Therefore, any living thing interacting with its environment should maintain the same constant ratio of Carbon-14 to Carbon-12 if it is alive. When it dies, it stops taking in Carbon-14 and the clock starts. Over time, the Carbon-14 decays and the ratio decreases. The measured ratio should then yield an indication of how long the organism has been dead.

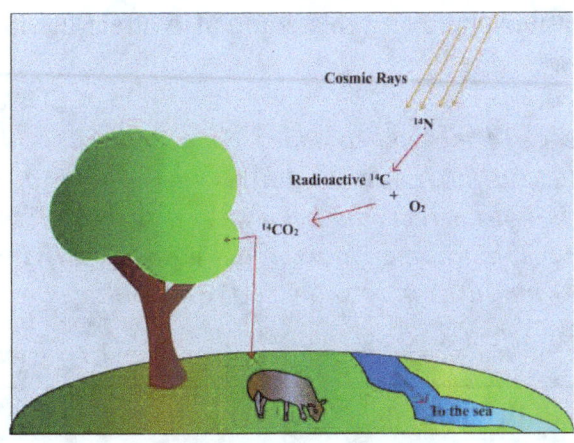

This method also has its problems. First, it assumes that the ratio of Carbon-14 to Carbon-12 in the environment is constant, but is it? Scientists generally accept that it would take about 30,000 years for the rate of buildup of Carbon-14 in the upper atmosphere to equal the rate of decay down here on earth. Dr. Libby himself noted that the production of Carbon-14 was as much as 25 percent higher than the rate of decay. He thought that it might be due to measuring error, but later measurements seem to support the discrepancy. What does this mean?

> *"The most reasonable conclusion from this fact is that the C-14/C-12 ratio is still building up in the world environment, because the required 30,000 years have not yet passed. In fact, this phenomenon of an increasing radiocarbon assay provides another very powerful means for estimating the age of the earth itself!"*[45]

Isn't that interesting? If the ratio is not constant in the environment, then it cannot be constant in living things and therefore we have a variable starting point on which to base the measurement. If the ratio is still building up, then organisms that died thousands of years ago when the ratio was even less would appear to be instantly old right after they died. We would also expect that many areas of the environment might not yet have caught up to even the present

---

45   Morris, *Scientific Creationism*, p. 165.

Because They Said So Isn't Good Enough

ratio in the atmosphere and this could also affect the ratio found in living things.

> "The C-14 method assumes the standard C-14/C-12 ratio applies to all living organisms at the time of death. That this is not correct has been shown in many instances. For example, it has been found that the shells of **living** (emphasis mine) mollusks may show radiocarbon ages of up to 2,300 years."[46]

> Wow, did you get that? How would you like to be told while you are still alive that you look like you have been dead for 2,300 years!

There is another problem. The rate of decay may not be constant. If the environment can influence other radioactive decays, why can't Carbon-14 decay be influenced as well? For that matter, how would we ever know? Remember the basin and salt analogy? Unless you can constantly watch the entire process, you will not know what external factors may influence your clock. The same thing can be said about the rate of Carbon-14 production. Did the bombardment of the atmosphere by cosmic radiation always remain constant? Again, how would we know? Man's recorded history only goes back some 6,000 years and we have only been able to measure radiation less than 200 years.

The method also cannot be used to verify incredibly old ages, the millions or billions of years often cited in the textbooks for the evolutionary ages. The half-life is too short, and the concentration of Carbon-14 is too low. After 5 half-lives, the total concentration of C-14 would be reduced to only 1/32 of the original amount ($\frac{1}{2} \times \frac{1}{2} \times \frac{1}{2} \times \frac{1}{2} \times \frac{1}{2}$). Such small concentrations would make it extremely difficult to accurately measure the ratio. Five half-lives represent less than 30,000 years, which is ridiculously small compared to the evolutionist's time scale.

---

[46] Ibid p. 162.

Interestingly, carbon 14 has been found in several samples of dinosaur bones. The specimens were gathered from all over: Texas, Alaska, Colorado, etc. In each case with careful adherence to procedure to avoid contamination, the bones yielded carbon 14 dates of less than 50, 000 years.[47] Hugh Miller and others authored a paper and presented the findings at a Geophysics meeting in Singapore in August of 2012. This is a huge problem because dinosaurs supposedly became extinct about 65 million years ago. It was so much of a problem that evolutionary scientists are now scrambling to squelch the findings. That is disappointing because as I indicated in chapter 1, science should be about changing our thinking when evidence is found contrary to our original hypothesis. It should never be about twisting, ignoring, or suppressing evidence. A proper response would be to repeat the test or seek corroborating evidence. If these tests are valid and I believe they are, then dinosaurs did not die out 65 million years ago but less than 50,000 years ago.

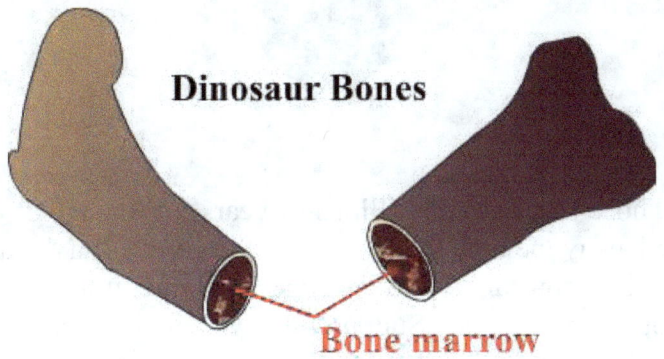

Dinosaur Bones

Bone marrow

Other Dating Methods

If we are really to be open-minded and scientific, should we not explore all other dating methods and see what they tell us as well? While some of these methods may also have problems, the overall picture they generate is probably more reliable than any one method alone. The following lists a few such methods and

---

47   Joe Spears MS, *Radiocarbon Dating of Dinosaur Fossils Triangle Association for the Science of Creation* (2013).

their conclusions. Interestingly, you do not hear of many of these discussed in the textbooks.

Decay of the earth's magnetic field – Over the last 170 years or so, we have measured the earth's magnetic field and found it to be decaying at an exponential rate. This fact was first made known by Dr. Thomas Barnes.[48] It has decreased about 7 percent from the initial measurements and that is a lot in so short a time. It is believed that the field is the result of electric current flowing in the earth's core. Based on the current decay rate, the conclusion was that that the earth cannot be old (less than 10,000 years) because the field strength would have been impossibly strong much beyond a few thousand years.

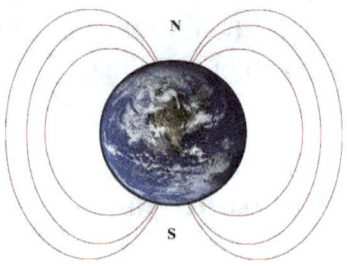

Those that favored billions of years for the age of the earth explained away the data by saying that the core was a dynamo; that the earth has constantly changed the field strength and direction continuously over time. Supposedly, we are just in one of the downward portions of one of the cycles. They cited the evidence in the rock formations for apparent reversals in the direction of the magnetic field. Does this theory, however, really explain the evidence?

First, the direction of the current flow would have to change to change the magnetic field. Such a change is not trivial and would require an enormous amount of energy. The existing field would also resist such a change. It would be like stopping the earth's rotation and then starting the earth's rotation in the opposite direction. Does

---

48   T. G. Barnes, "Decay of the earth's magnetic moment and the geochronological implications," in *Creation Research Society Quarterly 8* (1971), pp 24-29.

it really make sense that such a change can occur and that it did occur many times over long ages?

Dr. Russell Humphreys thinks there is a better explanation in keeping with Dr. Barnes original free-decay concept. He called it "dynamic-decay" and the idea is that the magnetic field has always decayed but that fluid flows in the earth's core may influence the field on the surface.[49] The concept is analogous to the Gulf Stream flowing up the coast of Florida. The general direction of the current is always the same, northward. Locally, however, the current can change direction several times a day. If tectonic shifts can cause tremendous effects on the water world we see (consider the recent tsunamis) is it so unreasonable to think that strong catastrophic events could also affect core fluids and explain the apparent magnetic field reversals? Dr. Humphreys seems to think so and concludes:

> *"At present, the only working theory for the origin, fluctuations, rapid reversals, and decay of the field is a creationist theory—a theory that fits all the data. Thus, according to the best theory and data we have, the earth's magnetic field certainly is less than 100,000 years old; very likely less than 10,000 years old and fits in well with the face-value Biblical age of 6,000 years."*[50]

Cometary Lifetimes – Comets are seen every year, and many are big events when they swing close enough for us to see them. Their orbits are elliptical reaching way out in space and then travel in close to the sun. It is that closeness to the sun that makes them spectacular nighttime viewing. The proximity to the sun is also the comet's undoing.

---

49   Russell Humphreys, Ph.D., "The Earth's Magnetic Field is Young," in *Impact No. 242* (Institute for Creation Research, 1993).
50   Humphreys, *The Earth's Magnetic Field is Young*, p. 2.

Every time a comet travels near the sun, a portion of the comets mass is blasted away by the solar radiation. Think of a racecar traveling on an oval track and every time the car passes the far turn a piece of the car falls off. It does not take a college graduate to realize the car can only make so many trips around the track before there is no more car. The same is true of comets. Astrophysicist Jason Lisle had this to say on the subject:

> *"A comet's tail (or tails) is an indication that comets cannot last forever. The tail means that the comet is losing material; a comet gets smaller every time it orbits the sun. It is estimated that a typical comet can only orbit the sun for about 100,000 years at most before completely running out of material. (This is an average figure, of course; the exact life span would depend on how big the comet is to begin with, and the parameters of its orbit.) Since we still have comets, this suggests that the solar system is much younger than 100,000 years."[51]*

> We still see comets. If the solar system is old and comets die quickly, then why are they still around?

Spiral Galaxy – Galaxies, particularly those that spiral, are very fascinating to view through our powerful telescopes. Astronomers have provided us with some nice pictures of many of them especially with the Hubble telescope. What many people do not think about, though, is the tremendous forces at work keeping them together.

---

51   Jason Lisle Ph.D. *Taking Back Astronomy* (Green Forest, AR: Master Books, 2016), p. 68.

David P. Mcintyre

Basically, according to Newton's third law an object will keep moving in a straight line unless acted upon by a force to change its path. For tight galaxy clusters, this force is gravity. This gravitational force would have to be incredibly large to hold the clusters together at the tremendous distances involved over the long-time periods claimed for the age of the universe. Such gravitation attraction must come from mass at or close to the center of the cluster. Many have postulated that this mass may be in the form of black holes that we cannot see because even light is prevented from escaping. Even though we may not be able to see such black holes, we should still be able to see their effect on nearby objects that we can see. If the mass is there, we should detect it. If we cannot, it is either well-hidden or not there. If it is missing, then how could the galaxies stay together for billions of years. They should have migrated apart long ago. If the universe is young, however, there simply has not been enough time for the stars to separate.

There is another problem as well. Things that spin tend to spin faster closer to the center and slower further out. Think of a tornado. The strongest winds are in the tightly wrapped cone and weakest further out from the center. If the galaxies are as old as claimed, the center of the spiral should be tightly wound (like the center of the tornado) but they are often not. It is an easy explanation if the universe is not old; there just has not been enough time passed for the spirals to tighten (like an early stage in the formation of a tornado). It is a lot more difficult to explain if the universe is old.

> *"Spiral galaxies slowly rotate, but the inner regions of the spiral rotate faster than the outer regions; this is called `differential rotation.` This means that a spiral galaxy is*

constantly becoming more and more twisted up as the spiral becomes tighter. After a few hundred million years, the galaxy would be wound so tightly that the spiral structure would no longer be recognizable. According to the big-bang scenario, galaxies are supposed to be billions of years old, yet we do see spiral galaxies – and lots of them. This suggests that they are not nearly as old as the big bang requires. Spiral galaxies are consistent with the biblical age of the universe but are problematic for a belief in billions of years."[52]

Sea Floor Mud – Every year rivers erode large amounts of rocks and dirt into the ocean. Only a small fraction of this material ever returns to land. Tectonic plate movement may take some of this away and push it under the continents but not all of it. A large percentage of the rocks and dirt simply stays in the ocean. If you keep throwing dirt into a hole over a long period of time eventually you start filling up the hole with dirt. Based on estimates of the average depth of the sediments on the ocean floor, the amount of sediments accumulated into the ocean each year, and the amount of sediments removed from the ocean, Dr. Russell Humphreys estimates the sediment could have been deposited in less than 12 million years.[53] It should be noted that many other such erosion and/or deposition phenomena such as the delta formations at the mouths of rivers also appear to point to much shorter time frames than the billions of years often quoted for the age of the earth.

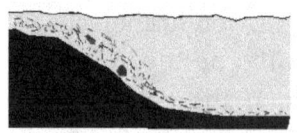 

Buildup Over Time

Degradation of Biological Material – DNA and proteins cannot last indefinitely in fossils. Eventually the complex molecules will degrade yet we still find such molecules in the fossils. Dr. Russell Humphreys suggests that these facts are powerful evidence

---

52   Lisle, *Taking Back Astronomy*, p. 66.
53   D. Russell Humphreys, Ph.D., *Impact #384: Evidence For a Young World* (El Cajon, CA: Institute for Creation Research, 2005), p. iii.

of a much younger earth.

> *"Natural radioactivity, mutations, and decay degrade DNA and other biological material rapidly. Measurements of the mutation rate of mitochondrial DNA recently forced researchers to revise the age of 'mitochondrial Eve' from a theorized 200,000 years down to possible as low as **6,000 years**. DNA experts insist that DNA cannot exist in natural environments longer than **10,000 years**, yet intact strands of DNA appear to have been recovered from fossils allegedly much older: Neanderthal bones, insects in amber, and even from dinosaur fossils. Bacteria allegedly 250 million years old apparently have been revived with no DNA damage. Soft tissue and blood cells from a dinosaur have astonished experts."*[54]

Recorded History – The most ancient records only go back about 5,000 to 6,000 years yet Homo sapiens have, supposedly, existed for more like 190,000 years according to the textbooks. Man has always sought immortality and what better way to obtain it than to find a way to record his deeds. If man is almost 200,000 years old than why did it take so long to find a way to record events?

I could go on about other evidences such as rates of accumulation of various elements into the ocean, river delta formation, carbon 14 found in deep rock strata, all of which indicate a much younger earth. They generally indicate a few million years at most. It is much easier, I believe, to conceive how long age indicators can be grossly in error (remember the salt basin analogy) then it is to explain how young age indicators can be "corrected" to indicate long ages.

One last thought needs to be discussed before concluding this subject…

---

54   Ibid p. iv.

The Speed of Light

One argument for long ages for the age of the universe is that it would take billions of years for light to reach the earth from very distant objects in space. Many have suggested that this is strong evidence the universe is old, but is it? There is no doubt that the distances are huge. They are in fact so large that we cannot measure the distance to many stars by the simple angular method used by surveyors. There are assumptions being made in the argument.

Assumption 1 – A young universe has a time problem, but old universe does not.

An old universe also has a time problem. The universe appears to be so vast that light cannot travel from one side of it to the other in the assumed age of the universe. If this is true than there should be detectable "hot" areas in some parts of the universe and "cold" regions in another. What scientists see, however, is that the temperature everywhere is the same. Let me use an analogy. If you were to heat up a pot of water to almost boiling and then add a block of ice into it, the water will eventually reach a temperature somewhere between the two extremes. Heat would flow from the hot water and melt the ice. If the two are in proximity, the transfer occurs rapidly. It would take more time if the hot water and the ice are widely separated. The energy transfer becomes even more difficult if the pot and the ice are moving away from each other. That is the case with the universe. It is expanding and apparently at a rate that it would be impossible for light energy traveling at the measured speed of light to travel from one side (point A) to the other (point B). Dr. Jason Lisle explains it this way:

> *"However, using the big-bang supporters' own assumptions (such as uniformitarianism and naturalism), there has not been enough time in 14 billion years to get light from A to B; they are too far apart."*[55]

---

[55] Lisle, *Astrophysics Taking Back* Astronomy, pp. 48-49

"The critic may suggest that the big bang is a better explanation of origins than the Bible since biblical creation has a light travel-time problem – distant starlight. Such an argument is not rational since the big bang has a light travel-time problem of its own. If both models have the same problem in essence, then that problem cannot be used to support one model over the other. Therefore, distant starlight cannot be used to dismiss the Bible in favor of the big bang."[56]

Assumption 2 – We know exactly how light responds as it travels through space

Granted, every time we measure the speed of light, we get the same result. Here is thought for consideration; how do we know that light acts the same over great distances as it does over the shorter distances? What if our assumptions about light are just approximations that work well over the short distances but not over exceptionally long distances? One thing I have learned about science is that our simple rules only work for a certain set of circumstances. Galileo many years ago wanted to see if heavier objects would fall faster than lighter ones. He took two rocks and dropped them from a tower, and they appeared to hit the ground at the same time. He concluded that objects fall at the same rate. Had he done the same experiment with a rock and a feather; the result might have been quite different. He might have concluded that heavier objects do fall faster. We now know that while the acceleration due to gravity is constant, other forces such as air resistance against a surface can influence the results. In science, many conclusions depend on doing the right measurements and carefully controlling anything that might artificially influence the result. When it comes to light, the right measurements may have to be measurements made over long distances and eliminate or minimize anything that might influence the light.

Consider this, if we wish to measure the speed of a car, we could lay out a course (say one mile) and then time how long the car takes to travel that distance. If it takes one minute, then the car

---
56   Ibid p. 50

is traveling at a mile a minute or 60 miles per hour. If we use the same course for light, it will appear to reach the end of the mile instantaneously. If we wanted to measure light for the same length of time our course would have to be 11.16 million miles long (186,000 miles/sec times 60 seconds). Most of our measurements about light, however, are made in extremely short distances. They are consistent, even reliable for predicting what will happen within say our own solar system, but can we really be sure that light acts the same way over extreme distances?

Some have speculated that light does not travel in a straight line over great distances but rather follows a curved path. If the light does follow a curved path, it could drastically alter our conclusions about how long it takes light to reach us. How could we tell which is correct? Again, it would require great distances out to the distance stars. If we observe our car traveling over a one-mile course, we could conclude that the car traveled in a straight line. It does not; it is traveling over the curvature of the earth. When the distance is small, though, we cannot detect it and for all practical purposes is traveling in a straight line. If the distance were increased, eventually we would notice the car dipping below the horizon as it travels on its curved path. As the circumference of our circle increases so must the distance we must measure to see the difference and draw a proper conclusion. If light does travel on a curved path, it would have to be on a huge curve perhaps closer to universe dimensions (e.g. light years). To prove that it did or did not travel in a straight line, we would have to extend our measurement out to the distant stars. At present we cannot do this and therefore we cannot absolutely prove which theory is correct.

A German mathematician by the name of Georg Friedrich Bernhard Riemann suggested a curved space geometry. What is interesting is the conclusion about how long it would take light to reach the earth if light traveled on a curved path (e.g. Riemannian surface). Harold Slusher had this to say on the subject:

> *"There is not much change between the two until the nearest star, Alpha Centauri, is reached. Consider the distance on a Riemannian surface of a star out on the edge of the observable universe at an infinite distance in Euclidean geometry. Upon taking the Euclidean distance as infinite, the distance to that star in Riemannian geometry according to the metric conversion is only 15.71 light years. That means if light travels on a Riemannian surface, it would take only 15.71 years of sidereal time to get from the farthest star to us...*[57]

I do not know which theory is correct or even that a different one may be true. The point is that we cannot be certain (if we ever can) until we are able to observe light over great distances. Until then, our speed of light measurement works fine for our solar system. We cannot be dogmatic that the universe is old based on straight-line geometry. We just do not know!

Albert Einstein

Albert Einstein handed the science community a new idea when he published his famous theory of relativity. He concluded that time is not always constant. Two factors can affect time for an object: the velocity of the object and its proximity to large concentrations of mass. Neither of these effects are large and can be ignored for life here on earth. The effects can be exceptionally large, though, when objects approach the speed of light or incredibly massive objects such as a black hole. Scientists began speculating that if a man were to travel into space and travel close to speed of light his time clock would slow down. If he traveled that way for a while and then came back to earth, he would perhaps age only a matter of weeks but those he left behind would have aged years or even died. Hefele and Keating decided to test the idea by putting atomic clocks on planes and flying them eastward around the earth and then westward. Theythen compared the time to a clock kept stationary on the ground at the US Naval Observatory. The clocks on

---

[57] Harold S. Slusher, *Age of the Cosmos*, pp. 36-37. (Note: The mathematical treatment and conversion equation can be found in Slusher's book between pages 33 and 37).

the planes responded as predicted by Einstein's theory and exhibited differences to the one on the ground.[58]

Einstein also theorized that time would slow down for an object nearer to a massive gravitational object such as a black hole. Sci-Fi movies and TV shows have capitalized on the idea. In Stargate SG-1 episode 15, a team was sent through the stargate to a distant world located close to a black hole. Time slowed down so much that they were not able to come back through the stargate before it had to be closed. Several experiments have been done to see if this effect is real. Atomic clocks have been placed at different altitudes. Those at lower altitudes (closer to the center of gravity) ticked slower than those at higher altitudes confirming Einstein's theory. Today's atomic clocks are so accurate that they can exhibit a minute difference when one clock is placed just 33 cm higher than the other.[59] If velocity and gravity have such an effect on time, what would time be like at the very beginning?

Discussion Points

- What are the problems with each assumption used in radiometric dating?

- Can carbon 14 be used to date old rocks? Explain.

- What do other dating methods such as the decay of the earth's magnetic field, the existence of comets, degradation of biological material in bones, etc. suggest about the age of the earth?

- Can we be certain that light from a distant star will take a long time (from our perspective) to reach the earth? Explain.

---

58 "Hafele-Keating Experiment,"
59 Ibid. "Hafele-Keating Experiment," Wikipedia.

Chapter 8 – Living Challenges

My brother Dennis read a draft of this book some time ago and suggested I add a chapter on some living things that are exceedingly difficult to explain in terms of evolution. There are many such examples and some readers may come up with many more. I have chosen 4 well documented examples: The Monarch butterfly, the salmon, the sea turtle, and bird flight. In each case, the question you should be asking is how these species could have developed with all their life characteristics through evolution.

Monarch Butterfly

The Monarch butterfly is found all over the United States, as far north as Michigan and New York and as far south as Florida. If you would like to view an excellent hour-long entertaining presentation on the butterfly and the Monarch in particular, I would highly recommend the video "Metamorphosis" available through Illustramedia.com. The facts I am presenting here have been taken from that video.

Life begins for the Monarch as an egg attached to the underside of a milkweed plant. The caterpillar emerging from the egg is totally different than the beautiful Monarch butterfly we later see. It is an eating machine that devours the milkweed leaves and grows to 3,000 times its initial weight in two weeks. The outer skin is built to stretch but it can only stretch so far and then must be shed and a new larger outer skin is produced. This molting process occurs four or five times in the two weeks. The milkweed plant is poisonous to predators of the Monarch butterfly. When the butterfly is mature, chemicals in the milkweed plant will be used to secrete an odor that helps keeps predators away. During the first two weeks, the caterpillar develops two types of cells: larval and imaginal. The larval are essentially the caterpillar; the imaginal cells will later develop into the mature butterfly.

When the caterpillar is big enough, it forms a chrysalis around itself. The larval cells die and become the raw materials that will be used to develop the imaginal cells into the mature butterfly. What is interesting is that the caterpillar cannot reproduce itself. Only the mature butterfly has reproductive capability. You cannot get to the mature butterfly, however, unless the caterpillar dies. How can any natural process explain such phenomena? The chrysalis is death to the caterpillar and the end of the species unless the caterpillar has been pre-programmed to build the butterfly that can reproduce. You cannot build this species or, for that matter, any butterfly by small changes over time. It is all or nothing. Inside it essentially dismantles itself, almost dies, and then rebuilds itself as an entirely different lifeform with none of the characteristics of the caterpillar. The transformation is amazing and beautiful. The video compares the transformation to a model T car that after driving a bit builds a garage around itself. Then it dismantles itself completely and rebuilds itself into a sophisticated helicopter. How does that happen by chance?

That is not the whole story. After the butterfly emerges, mating occurs and the female lays eggs on the underside of another milkweed to begin a new cycle. The normal life cycle from egg to mature butterfly to death is about 2-4 weeks. In the fall when the temperature drops in the northern states, the milkweed goes dormant. The Monarch butterfly senses the change and feeds heavily on nectar to build up its reserves. That generation is the methuselah generation. It will live up to 9 months. It will then undertake up to a 2,500-mile journey from all over the United States and Canada to a specific trans-volcanic mountain range in Mexico. It will spend 8 weeks flying averaging 50 miles per day. The Monarch butterfly will sense the suns position and know the time of day from an internal clock to help it navigate. When it gets close to its destination, magnetite in the Monarch will act like a compass to help locate the specific target due to a higher concentration of heavy metals in the area.

    Multiple millions of these butterflies will congregate on the tall evergreen pines in the area and there they will winter. The temperature remains in a range that can be tolerated. The butterflies essentially hibernate. When spring comes, the butterflies seek out nectar to refill their energy tanks. When the first milkweed plants appear in Texas, they head toward the plants, lay eggs and die. The next generation will follow the milkweed plants as they appear, and the monarchs gradually move north until fall when a new methuselah generation appears to make the trek back to Mexico. Wow! How can all this ever happen by a blind undirected process?

Because They Said So Isn't Good Enough

Pacific Salmon

The following facts were taken from Illustra Media video, "Living Waters".[60]

The salmon begins life in a shallow stream well up into a river. After hatching it will need more resources to grow and so it makes its way down the river to saltwater. It must adapt to the saltwater environment. As it makes its way downstream sensors for the earth's electromagnetic field and a sense of smell creates an imprint map which years later will be used to guide the salmon back to the very shallow stream where it was born. When it makes the journey, the salmon uses the earth's magnetic field to locate the mouth of the right river. From then on it will sample the water and smell its way back to the precise stream bed. There is an incredible bioengineering system involved here. More than half a million cells test the waters looking for key chemical agents in the water. When the right agent is sensed, it triggers a signal cascade to nerve cells, to biological wires to a processor which organizes the data and compares it to the prerecorded memory map the salmon created as it worked its way down the river to the ocean. The salmon then spends the next 17 days following the chemical trail without eating until it reaches the exact small bed where it was born. Millions of salmon repeat the process every year.

The question here is how such a complex navigation system could ever happen by chance. According to evolution a fish is not high up on the ladder from simple to complex biological species. How then could it develop such an incredibly sensitive system. There is no advantage to the salmon until it is fully developed. There may not be even any pressure to develop such a system. The salmon

---
60   Illustra Media, "Living Waters," DVD

could mate and lay eggs anywhere. The quiet protected waters of a shallow stream with few predators might provide the best place to hatch new salmon and give them the best chance at initial survival. An all wise creator/designer might provide the salmon with the biological guidance system to accomplish the task. Chance would be indifferent and would not.

Sea Turtle

The following facts were taken from Illustra Media video, "Living Waters".[61]

The sea turtle begins its life on a sandy beach. After hatching, the small turtle is smaller than the hand of a child and quickly makes its way to the water. It then must swim hard for the next 2 days to avoid predators and make its way well out into the open ocean. Somehow, though, as it swims it uses the earth's magnetic field to create a map of its journey much like an electronic GPS. The turtle will make its way to feeding grounds that may be more than a thousand miles away and stay away for years as it matures. When it comes time to mate, the females will use the imprinted map to guide its journey back to the precise beach where it was hatched. Then after laying its eggs it will make the journey back to the same feeding grounds a thousand or more miles away. The journey may be made several times during the turtle's lifetime; the lifespan is typically over 50 years.

Again, the question here is how this complex navigation system could ever just happen by chance. Without it the turtle would never find its way back to either the beach or the feeding grounds. The same is true if it is only partially developed. If the turtle can

---

61   Ibid. *Illustra Media,* "Living Waters,"

recognize the changes in the earth's magnetic field but does not know how to interpret it, the turtle will be lost. If it can sense the changes and interpret it but has no memory storage, the turtle is still lost. If it has memory but cannot sense or interpret anything it is still lost. All the elements must be present at the same time to work. This incredible turtle had GPS tracking long before man ever even thought of it. It also appears that many other species including butterflies, birds, fish etc. also have the ability. This is precisely what we would expect from a master designer, God, but not from chance mutations. The system would not give any advantage to the turtle until it was fully formed, and functional and so natural selection would not give any preference to a turtle with a partially developed system.

David P. Mcintyre

Bird Flight

There are some 9,000 species of birds, most capable of flight. We see so many flying around that we hardly think about what it takes to allow them to fly. They are marvels of engineering. The bone structure is designed to provide maximum strength for the least amount of weight. The muscles are placed to flap the wings most efficiently. The heart often beats at 500 or more times per minute to supply the needed oxygen to the muscles. The lungs are among the most efficient in the animal world. Some of the feathers interlock to provide an airfoil to create lift while others can be moved independently to control movement and direction or serve as air brakes to slow forward motion when landing. All the parts are assembled inside the egg and after a few short weeks the baby bird is ready to take its solo flight. Somehow the bird knows exactly what to do. It is an all or nothing system. Any part that does not work properly and the bird will not fly and will likely die. How does such a system happen by chance? If you would like to see an incredible video on the subject, I would recommend the video "Flight".[62] The following examples have been taken from that video.

Hummingbirds

These tiny birds are nature's helicopters. They flap their wings a hundred times a second. They are capable of incredible aerobatics. The wings flap up and down when flying forward but flap in a figure eight pattern to hover. They can even fly backwards. Their heart beats at over a thousand beats per minute and they must consume twice their body weight every day. Even their long tongue is specially designed to maximize the extraction of nectar from flowers. They are tiny, beautiful marvels of engineering. What process could possibly produce these gradually?

---

62 *Illustra Media*, "Flight," DVD

Starlings

These small birds cluster in large groups of 200,000 or more individual birds. They travel as much as 30 miles away from their nests to feed. The large flock helps to ward off or confuse predators. They fly in close formation to each other, but each bird continuously monitors the birds closest to it. If any bird moves, those closest to it also move. Each bird then individually signals the whole flock to change. The whole flock moves as if it was one organism. The result is an incredible aerial display that boggles the mind. It could almost be put to music. (The "Flight" video captures some of these movements.) Even though they fly remarkably close to each other, the birds never crash into each other. Such actions require a flying precision that no human could ever match.

The Artic Turn

This bird has the longest migration pattern of any bird. It spends most of its life in the air. It nests in the artic in the summer and when the temperature drops the birds will fly all the way to Antarctica. When the temperature drops there, they will fly all the way back to the very nesting grounds they came from. They will make this 24,000-mile round trip as many as 30 times in their lifetime. Some scientists attached small GPS trackers to a few of the birds and then recovered about 20 percent of them the following year when they returned to the nesting grounds. The purpose was to map out the flight patterns. Going south half of the birds flew along the coast of Africa and the other half flew along Brazil. On the return flight, however, they all followed an S shaped path northward to the same nesting grounds. These birds used the Sun's position, the position of the stars and the earth's magnetic field to accurately navigate the trip.

We do not have to go far to find evidence of design in nature. It is all around us. It is so prevalent that evolutionary scientists must remind people that what they are seeing is not designed. I would beg to differ; what we are seeing is precisely evidence of a master designer at work.

David P. Mcintyre

"For the wrath of God is revealed from heaven against all ungodliness and unrighteousness of men, who suppress the truth in unrighteous, because what may be known of God is manifest in them for God has shown it to them. For since the creation of the world His invisible attributes are clearly seen, being understood by the things that are made, even His eternal power and Godhead, so that they are without excuse" (Rom 1:18-20)

Discussion Points

- Check which of the following living challenges you believe are possible by mutations and natural selection. Explain.

    - Monarch Butterfly
    - Pacific Salmon
    - Sea Turtle
    - Flight
    - Starlings
    - Hummingbird
    - Artic Turn

Chapter 9 – Put It All Together

So far, we have examined several aspects of the question of origins. Your brain must be hurting. This is heavy stuff. Let's put all of the pieces together by answering the question raised in each chapter from my perspective, simply and to the point:

- Chapter 1 - *Evolution Fact or Faith*? Faith, because no one was there to observe it.
- Chapter 2 - *Life: How Complex Is the Problem*? The odds are so far beyond even what scientists say is possible so I would answer impossible.
- Chapter 3 - *Overcoming the Odds Does Nature Really Have the Tools*? No, they are woefully inadequate.
- Chapter 4 - *Aren't There Proofs That Evolution Is True*? No, there are many people saying it is true yet simply saying something is true does not make it true.
- Chapter 5 - *I Heard They Created Life in The Laboratory*. No, not even close, and any success was due to highly intelligent people controlling every step of the experiments.
- Chapter 6 - *All Those Fossils Prove Evolution Is True Don't They*? No, in fact they are more consistent with a creation view and a catastrophic event, like Noah's flood.
- Chapter 7 - *Dating and Time*. Radiometric dating is unreliable except perhaps for short ages. There are many indicators that the earth, solar system, even the universe is not that old.
- Chapter 8 - *Living Challenges*. Many living things cannot be explained in terms of a random evolutionary process. They undeniably declare to me that they were created by an incredibly masterful, brilliant designer. They remind me of the words in Romans *1:20*.

"For since the creation of the world His invisible attributes are clearly seen, being understood by the things that are made, even His eternal power and Godhead so that they are without excuse."

Because They Said So Isn't Good Enough

The journey has driven me to acknowledge the Creator God and to learn whatever I can about Him.

David P. Mcintyre

Epilogue – A Different Perspective from Genesis 1

A Lot in One Verse…

This portion admittedly is going to get a little spiritual. For those of you who are not so inclined, you could skip it. I think it would be a mistake, however, as you will miss out on some real insight into the creation perspective. It really isn't that long anyway. So please read on...

Have you ever noticed that whenever we read often the first words do not register? It takes a while for our brain to tune into what is being said. If you are like me, I read several sentences or even paragraphs before I begin to understand. The best authors know this tendency and spend an inordinate amount of time on the first few sentences. They are trying to draw us in. Those first words set the tone, paint a picture and, if possible, touch our emotions. If we are open to them, they will embrace us. We often do not fully appreciate those first words until the whole book has been read. Then when we reread those first words, the message leaps out of the page and perhaps the whole book is then remembered by those first words we so quickly glossed over in the beginning. I believe the first two chapters of Genesis are like this as well....

I would like to look at the first verse in Genesis from a different perspective.

"In the beginning, God created the heavens and the earth." (Genesis 1:1)

I have read several books by Dr. Henry M. Morris who gave me great insight in Genesis 1:1. I will give him credit for the insights but let me put it in my own words.

I am not a Hebrew scholar, so I rely on Strong's Exhaustive Concordance of the Bible[63] to help me dig deeper into the original Bible words and their meaning. According to Strong's, the Hebrew word translated "God" in Genesis 1:1 is "Elohiym". The interesting thing is that the word is plural not singular indicating more than one. The Hebrew word "bara" translated created, however, is singular. We have a plural noun with a singular verb. The plural entity is then acting as one (e.g. a plural God acting with a singular purpose). Suppose I was to say:

---

63   James Strong, *The Exhaustive Concordance of The Bible* (McLean, VA: MacDonald Publishing Company, 22102).

"The Sunday school class is going to do a play".

In this case, the class (plural) is operating as a unity and this is exactly analogous to the structure in Genesis 1:1. God is a unity of more than one! There is further confirmation of this in Genesis 1:26:

"And God said, let us make man in our image, after our likeness...."

Again, God is more than one. We are not told how many make up the unity but there is more than one. We have a clue to how many, though, in what is created. The created world of Genesis 1:1 is made up of:

1. **Time** - "In the beginning"
2. **Space** - "the heavens"
3. **Matter** - "the earth"

There are three parts and as we will learn later in the Scriptures, God is also three in one. There is God the Father, God the Son and God the Holy Spirit. Genesis 1:1 is the first hint at a triune Godhead!

There is more. We cannot describe any of the parts of the creation (time, space and matter) without invoking the other two. Time, for example, is described in terms of the hands of a clock (matter) moving around the clock face (space). If you wish to refer to a piece of matter, you must describe its location in space at a moment in time. Even space is meaningless unless occupied by matter existing in time. All the parts go together, but each is distinct. No one confuses time with space or space with matter or matter with time. Yet each occupies the entire universe. Where does time leave off and space begin? It doesn't! Time is throughout the universe. The entire universe is made up of space. The whole thing contains matter.

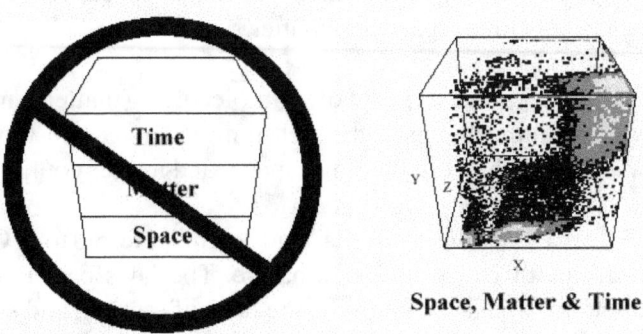

Space, Matter & Time

What a beautiful analogy to the Triune Godhead! God the Father is everywhere, so is the Son and so is the Holy Spirit. Yet each is separate. Yet we cannot describe any one of them without talking about the other two. God the Father sends the Son to die for our sins (John 3:16) and draws all men to Himself through the work of the Holy Spirit. The Son points to the Father and sends the Holy Spirit to comfort us. The Holy Spirit points to the Son to fulfill the will of the Father. Incredible! Notice the entire Godhead is centered on you and me! God the Father is trying to bridge the gap to sinful man through the atoning death of the Son and the promptings of the Holy Spirit to trust, to believe. Three in one Godhead just like the three in one created universe!

There is still more. The concept of time, space and matter is the basis of all science. If we try to talk about motion, for example, you will study how matter moves through space in a certain amount of time.

Consider Einstein's famous equation equating matter and energy:

$$E = mc^2$$

The "m" stands for mass, a measure of matter. The "c" is the speed of light, a measure of distance (space) traveled in a certain amount of time.

If you really want to measure heat, you describe the motion of particles traveling through space.

Electricity is electrons (matter) moving through wires (space) at a moment in time.

The forces of gravity involve a measure of matter accelerating toward each other. Again, it is time, space and matter.

Even the biological processes involve molecules (matter) moving, colliding, and combining in space through time to invoke all biological changes. Life itself is subject to the time, space, and matter continuum.

That is not all! If we study the "heavens" and "earth" referred to in Genesis 1:1, we find still another clue to God's nature. The laws based on time, space and matter (e.g. the law of gravity, the laws of motion, and so forth) do not change. They are so reliable we can confidently send someone to the moon and back. We can bounce signals off satellites to receivers to our TV sets and bring programs consistently to our homes. We can create reliable electric power we can all use. We confidently walk out to our cars expecting them to consistently perform for us. We even look to the most distant parts of the universe and find that even there the laws appear to operate the same. That... is.... amazing! No evolution model would predict these phenomena! Why should everything evolve the same way or abide by the same rules? For that matter, why should there be any rules?

It says a lot, though, about a Creator God. He is consistent. He is reliable. He does not change. We can trust Him.

Those that read the Bible often miss the meaning of those first words, just ten words. They tell us a lot about God and lay the foundation for the whole rest of the Bible. Let me just give a few points to think about:

- If God created the entire universe, He must be an incredible all-powerful being. Is anything, anything at all too hard for Him?

- If He can create the universe, can He not also in His time repair it? Is then any problem we might have too hard for Him to solve?

- If He can create time, how then can time bind Him? Would He not know all? Would He not have a plan to repair a world gone astray because of man?

- If He can create the heavens, can He not also create a place for us?

- If He created matter with such consistent, reliable properties, is not this creation a testimony to a consistent reliable God?

- If the created life has incredible complexity, diversity and at the same time interdependency, is He not showing us how valuable we all are and how valuable each of us is to the whole?

- If each part of the creation (time, space, matter) cannot be spoken of without speaking of the other two, does this not speak of a God who is intimately interested and involved in others including us?

- As we ponder the mind of a simple man who pours his energy and love into an object he has made and then look at the breathtaking beauty of God's creation, cannot we see God's infinite love?

Then He tells me how to live forever in His love.

He tells me I am a sinner. I knew that.

> "*For all have sinned and fall short of the glory of God*" (Romans 3:23)

He says the pay for sin is death. Ouch!

> "*For the wages of sin is death, but the gift of God is eternal life in Christ Jesus our Lord.*" (Romans 6:23)

The latter part of that verse gives me hope, that God has worked it out in His love.

> "*But God demonstrates His own love toward us, in that while we were still sinners, Christ died for us.*" (Romans 5:8)

I have only to respond and accept His gift.

> "*For God so loved the world that He gave His only begotten Son, that whoever believes in Him should not perish but have everlasting life.*" (John 3:16)

Dear reader, you may believe something different. If you turn out to be correct, I will simply die having lived a delusion all these years. I will be no worse off. If God created the world however, and the words of the Bible are true, where will your faith take you?

"He who believes in the Son has everlasting life; and he who does not believe the Son shall not see life, but the wrath of God abides on him." (John 3:36)

I urge you to choose life.